Quiet
MOMENTS
for worship leaders

SCRIPTURES,

MEDITATIONS,

& PRAYERS

MARTY PARKS

BEACON HILL PRESS
OF KANSAS CITY

Copyright 2008
by Marty Parks and Beacon Hill Press of Kansas City

ISBN 978-0-8341-2372-4

Printed in the
United States of America

Cover Design: Darlene Filley
Interior Design: Sharon Page

Library of Congress Cataloging-in-Publication Data

Parks, Marty.
    Quiet moments for worship leaders : scriptures, meditations, and prayers / Marty Parks.
       p. cm.
    ISBN 978-0-8341-2372-4 (pbk.)
    1. Bible. O.T. Psalms—Devotional use. I. Title.

    BS1430.54.P37 2008
    242'.69—dc22

                                                                2008014274

10 9 8 7 6 5 4 3 2 1

CONTENTS

INTRODUCTION

Does the Christian world really need another daily devotional book? Does the ancient Book of Psalms really need one more expository treatment? Does any one of us really need more stuff to clutter our bookshelves or one more daily obligation to cram into our already over-committed lives?

Probably not. However, experience has taught me that when I neglect God's Word, when I'm too noisy to hear Him, when I'm too frantic to just "be," I'm the one who loses out. I'm afraid I've learned this the hard way.

On the other hand, when I allow God's Word to penetrate me, when I'm still enough to listen, when I invite quietness and confidence in His Word into my life, I find I'm infused with strength, trust, and encouragement for the day. And who among us couldn't use a little more of that?

Of course, this isn't my original thought. The ageless collection of writings we call the Psalms prods us over and over to meditate on God's law, to delight in His precepts, to rejoice in His statutes. In all of these we find life as it's meant to be lived. Refreshingly honest, these words of David, Moses, Asaph, and others remind me of how gritty our existence can be. I relate to these men—their passion for worship, their love of God's Word, and, unfortunately, their colossal failures. There's warmth and comfort in these utterances. There's also plenty to make us squirm with conviction. Most of all, when we consider the Psalms all together, we're driven to the one who inspired them in the first place.

So, pastors, worship leaders, and all those following hard after God (see Ps. 63:8), I invite you to plunge in with me as we soak ourselves in the water of God's truth. I so look forward to joining you for a few minutes each day as we're moved to praise, adoration, confession, and thanksgiving through the direction of our original Book of worship.

Take your time. Be intentional about being open. Breathe in His Word. Listen closely.

1
TRUE SIGNIFICANCE

Psalm 1

His delight is in the law of the LORD,
and on his law he meditates day and night.
—Ps. 1:2

If my life is going to count, if I'm to make a difference in my world, then I'll walk with those who can build up my faith. I'll concentrate on the law of God—all His precepts.

If you're at all like me, you can do without the distraction of critical, negative, or indifferent people in your life. You don't need to listen to those who try to persuade you with every new intellectual fad or spiritual philosophy that comes along. Life is challenging—and so "daily," as some put it—that sometimes it's only because of the grounding I receive in God's Word and the delight that comes to me through His promises that I'm able to make it at all! Sound familiar?

Today we begin a trek through the ancient Book of Psalms, Israel's original hymn book and the world's greatest worship treasury. The Psalms open with a benediction and the word "blessed." The actual Hebrew word used here for "blessed" is *'esher*. It indicates happiness sort of as an exclamation, as in "How happy!" It implies happiness that bubbles over into every aspect of life, so much so that others can't help but notice. Interestingly, this word is closely related to and is actually derived from another Hebrew word, *'ashar*, meaning "to be straight or level; to go forward; to be honest—to prosper."

I would like to think my life is marked by some type of significance—in my work, my relationships, and my family. We probably all yearn for happiness and for prosperity, but deep inside, don't you long for life to really count for something? I'm finding that happiness and prosperity are the inevitable byproducts of a life rooted and established in God's Word—not happiness and prosperity as the world defines them, but characteristics that grow in us as God orders our attitudes and increases our hunger not only for His Word but also for Him. And in Him is our true significance.

Prayer: *God, please fill me fresh again with your Spirit, and plant me firm in your Word. Help my relationships be significant and my worship authentic. In Christ's name I pray. Amen.*

Thought for the Day: We will be called truly blessed when we've drunk from the "fount of every blessing."

2
WELL PLANNED—
WE THOUGHT

Psalm 2
Blessed are all who take refuge in him.
—Ps. 2:12

God must laugh sometimes at our plans. He's probably somewhere between amused and frustrated when we try to define or control Him. Though we can know His character, we cannot predict what He'll do.

Too many times I've entered into a season of worship and I've attempted it all in my own strength. The energy level may have been high, the song list stellar, and the overall sound spectacular. But I was left feeling a little flat, like something—or *someone*—was missing. The fact is, in times like these, if God doesn't show up, I'm sunk!

Submission to His direction and prompting is what makes my life and my worship profitable—pleasing in God's eyes. I think that's what the writer of Ps. 2 had in mind when, in verse 7, he refers to God as Father and himself as son. In the ancient culture that birthed this psalm, submission of a servant to a king was often expressed in father/son terms. In the best of situations, the father's authority and power were extended to the privileged son.

All this, of course, is Messianic in nature and gives us an insightful, prophetic portrait of the relationship of Jesus to His Father. Still, there's lots here we can learn about submitting to and actually pleading for our Father's direction and plan for us. Those plans may not look like anything we would ever dream or imagine, but who among us is content to attempt only the things we can do on our own?

Prayer: *Father, we cry out for your protection and your direction. We pay homage, offer reverence, and submit our will to your Son, our Savior. In His name we pray. Amen.*

Thought for the Day: Submitting to God means gaining His authority.

3
THE BATTLES AROUND ME

Psalm 3

You are a shield around me, O LORD;
you bestow glory on me and lift up my head.
—Ps. 3:3

One of the more difficult things I attempt is relying fully on God. I tend to trust my professional abilities, my creative prowess, or my people skills when I should be trusting God.

My Bible ascribes Ps. 3 to David, and the subtitle states that he wrote it "when he fled from his son Absalom." The full story of this dysfunctional season in David's family life can be read in 2 Sam. 15—17. If you're not familiar with the story, brace yourself as you read. Try to see beyond the printed page and into the raw emotion that must have accompanied the events depicted there: treachery, betrayal, a wayward son, an attempted coup. Israel's family therapists could have had a field day!

Mutiny or betrayal is ugly, no matter the circumstances. When it includes close friends or family, the wounds are even deeper, aren't they? It's amazing how David handled insults, curses, and even threats on his life during this period. First of all, he claims God as his shield, his close and immediate source of protection. Next, he refers to God as his glory, which, according to the original Hebrew word, implies "to be heavy; to make weighty with honor; to be honorable; rich." Finally, he calls God his *Ruwm Rosh*—the One who lifts my head.

Though I've not received any threat on my life—*yet*—sometimes I do feel like a battle's raging with all those around me. I want to handle personal attacks, insults, and criticism the way David did. When cursed, he looked beyond the words and even the person hurling the curses. He considered the words against him for what they were worth, analyzed them for any possible truth, then discarded the rest. To do this in the midst of great disloyalty and revolt takes an extra measure of grace, wisdom, and peace. Ultimately, when he was running for his life, David relied fully on God, the only one who could make him lie down, sleep, and wake again due to His sustaining and loyal love.

Prayer: *O God, help me to be one whose demeanor and influence discourages deception and disloyalty. Nothing can be accomplished if I'm suspicious of others. Help me not give in to idle chatter, gossip, or backbiting. May my thoughts and words honor you. In Jesus' name I pray. Amen.*

Thought for the Day: God alone is my shield, my glory, and the lifter of my head.

4

MERCY AND LOVE

Psalm 5

I, by your great mercy, will come into your house;
in reverence will I bow down toward your holy temple.
—Ps. 5:7

Personally, Ps. 5 is an ideal one for me. I resonate with "in the morning," and "by your great mercy," and the references to God's favor. There's something about beginning the day with a word from God that helps put the rest of my day into perspective.

When my first thoughts in the morning are centered on Him, I see Him throughout the day in even the little things. Mostly, this is because I've been reminded to be looking. Psalm 143 is closely related to this sentiment, as we read in verse 8—"Let the morning bring me word of your unfailing love, for I have put my trust in you." I can't begin to count the mornings I've desperately needed to cling to His unfailing love, to hold fast to His great mercy, to bow—if not my whole body then my whole heart—before His throne.

God's great mercy and unfailing love are recurring themes throughout the Psalms. I suspect that's because an ever-benevolent Father knew we would need reminding. He knew we would become wrapped up in our own real or imagined conflicts. He's all too aware of how we slip into self-protection mode when attacked, whether we're truly innocent or we've brought it on ourselves. And He's keenly conscious that only He can provide for the two things all of us need most—great mercy and unfailing love.

Yes, I'm sure He knew we would need the reminder, over and over, morning by morning. And if we follow King David's lead, we'll lay our requests before Him and wait in expectation, knowing He'll hear us, knowing He's waiting for us. After all, He invited us.

Prayer: *Loving Father, how wonderful to meet you early in the morning, to watch the day unfold in your presence! In your Son's name I pray. Amen.*

Thought for the Day: Focusing on God's attributes brings confidence.

5
SPEAKING TO GOD

Psalm 7

I will give thanks to the LORD because of his righteousness
and will sing praise to the name of the LORD Most High.
—Ps. 7:17

Let's get one thing clear from the beginning: I do not know what a "shiggaion" is. I'm not sure I can even pronounce it correctly. Highly esteemed biblical scholars aren't quite certain either. Yet there it is—just below the chapter heading "Psalm 7" and apparently written by David. *Shiggaion* seems to be one of those terms we find in the Psalms—like *Maskil* or *Miktam*—about which we're left to speculate. I'm guessing it's a musical term, but we just don't know.

Sometimes I think God leaves us wondering about things like this—or like some of the musical instruments mentioned in Scripture—so that we, in our feeble attempt to define "proper" worship style, wouldn't be tempted to say, "This psalm *must* be sung to this tune, and it *must* be accompanied by this instrument, and it *must* be used only for this occasion."

Instead, we're left with only the term *shiggaion* itself and a description of what David did with it. And that's the point! Psalm 7 was something David sang *to* the Lord—not about Him or in reference to Him but actually *to* Him. God, in His infinite wisdom, has omitted any explanations of style or form, and nowhere will we find any semblance of a divine order of worship. Maybe that's so our response to Him will be personal, honest, and truly intimate.

I'm convinced that God honors our honesty in both prayer and in worship. How often my mind and spirit have wandered in both endeavors! Has that ever happened to you? You may be encouraged to know that one meaning for the phrase "I take refuge in you" (v. 1) indicates "confiding in." It's hard to confide in anyone when we're only partially engaged. A full-on interaction is what God invites.

It's not about the form or the melody or the musical instruments. It's about an open, honest dialog. And if we listen carefully, we'll hear Him respond.

Prayer: *Lord, today I want to speak to you, sing to you, respond to you. And I'll listen for your word to me. Thank you for the joy and comfort of confiding in you. In Christ's name I pray. Amen.*

Thought for the Day: Speaking to God is an integral part of my relationship with Him.

6
AN EVERYWHERE GOD

Psalm 8

What is man that you are mindful of him, the son of man
that you care for him?
—Ps. 8:4

In many ways, Ps. 8 is a natural follow-up to Ps. 7. In both I'm reminded that there really is only one source of true, unfailing, dependable protection—the Most High God! I'm amazed that this magnificent, sovereign Creator is mindful of me—of you. His glory is revealed in creation, yet He's taken the deliberate action to stoop and make himself known to us. If we're watching, we'll see Him everywhere. He is totally astounding, and I want to know Him more.

I imagine that David composed Ps. 8 while he was still shepherding his father's flocks, long before he became Israel's king. Perhaps it was a crisp, cool, starry night, and the brilliance of the universe above and around him moved him deeply. Almost unthinkable was—and is—the reality that the cosmic designer would be so aware of His human creation that He would crown him with glory and honor and give him dominion over creation. And if that were not enough, He has not only ordained praise but also dwells in it. (See Ps. 22:3, KJV.)

David ascribes majesty to God's name in verse 1. No doubt he understood that the names by which God has chosen to reveal himself speak volumes about His character, His essence. Think for a moment about every name for God you can recall. What does each one mean to you? Which one is closest to you right now?

I love the words of Henry van Dyke that we know from the classic hymn "Joyful, Joyful, We Adore Thee:"

> All Thy works with joy surround Thee;
> Earth and heav'n reflect Thy rays.
> Stars and angels sing around Thee,
> Center of unbroken praise.

May it ever be so in your life and mine.

Prayer: *Sovereign Lord, eternal Father, matchless Creator, I stand in awe of one so great. I bow in humility and gratitude to one who has revealed himself to me. I offer my life as one small part of a universe that explodes in your praise. In Jesus' name I pray. Amen.*

Thought for the Day: All creation is an outstretched finger pointing to God.

7

PRAISE BEFORE OUR BATTLES

Psalm 9

Those who know your name will trust in you, for you, LORD,
have never forsaken those who seek you.
—Ps. 9:10

There's something about praising God that not only attracts people but also turns away evil. When we recount the deeds of God and proclaim His incredible greatness, I'm certain that the enemy of our souls is shaken. That's one of the vital aspects of worship—Satan is brought down when God is lifted up in unity.

Yesterday we reflected on some of the names of God, and you were encouraged to list some of those most meaningful to you. I'm pretty sure David engaged in this practice from time to time. I can almost see him diligently creating a list of descriptive titles for the God he knew so well. Sometimes he would write them down in tender gestures. At other times only bold strokes of his pen could convey the weightiness of a name.

Here, in verse 9, he calls on *Jehovah Mishgabbi,* The Lord My Stronghold. That sort of assurance in a name is accompanied by comfort, strength, and security. And I just imagine that God himself is delighted when we, like David, express our total confidence in Him.

It's quite possible that David was also reviewing his history lessons a bit. It's very likely that he was taking his cues from one of Israel's earlier kings, Jehoshaphat, who responded to the very real threat of an enemy's attack not by consultation with the secretary of war, not by convening a meeting with the joint chiefs of staff, not even by mustering the warriors and preparing for combat. Instead, he organized a choir to go out proclaiming the greatness of God! For the results and full account of this unusual strategy, read 2 Chron.

20, remembering that for Jehoshaphat, for David, for you and for me, praise goes before the battle.

Prayer: *Lord, many times I feel surrounded by enemies that threaten my life in physical and spiritual ways. These attackers presume to destroy my very relationship with you. At these times, Father, be my refuge, my stronghold, my comfort, and my deliverer. And I, like David, will praise you forever and ever. In your Son's name I pray. Amen.*

Thought for the Day: God has always protected His worshipers.

8

EXCELLENCE IN HIS EYES

Psalm 10

Why, O LORD, do you stand far off?
Why do you hide yourself in times of trouble?
—Ps. 10:1

At times, it seems that God is unconcerned with our trials. Until we realize just how many of them are of our own making!

Following the "arrogance of man" (v. 2) is always trouble, and it's totally deceptive. Leaning on that kind of understanding does not make for a straight path. Admitting our dire weakness is the first step to claiming the promise of *Jehovah Ozer Li*—God, my Helper.

We live in a celebrity culture. The entertainment industry supplies us each season with dozens of rising stars, most of whom we'll have forgotten in an incredibly short amount of time. Even the medical and legal professions have produced—or manufactured—their own brand of celebrity on a local, national, and even international level. What once were honorable but relatively obscure occupations now boast billboards, broadcasts, and best-sellers.

Our churches can fall prey to this mind-set. Bigger buildings, the latest programming, better technology, and engaging platform personalities can all vie for our attention as we compare our congregation and our mission to other fellowships. Arrogance often cloaks itself as a desire for "excellence." But when excellence becomes the goal, or when worship itself takes precedence over the *object* of our affection and the *subject* of our devotion—Jesus Christ—then we've been deceived, caught in the schemes of arrogance.

Prayer: *O God, you are the only thing excellent in my life. Heal me of pride and arrogance, and remind me that you alone are my helper. In Christ's name I pray. Amen.*

Thought for the Day: Standing on our own is a sure way to fall.

9
WORSHIP'S FIRST PRIORITY

Psalm 11

He observes the sons of men; his eyes examine them.

—Ps. 11:4

I want to get to the point where I stop trusting in my abilities or gifts, and I stop worrying about others' perception of me. I want my life to be defined by trusting in God.

That's a tall order for many of us who have spent a good part of our lives serving in local congregations. While ministering is an important responsibility, our first obligation is to God. In this day of consumer-oriented church programming and cafeteria-styled worship, responding to what people want can be a tough obstacle. Still, the biblical record indicates that Israel's priests were called primarily to minister to the Lord.

I'm encouraged by David's reminder that God observes and examines *us* (v. 4)—not our productivity or accomplishments. That phrase has interesting connotations in the original Hebrew. It means "to perceive, to behold (as in take in fully), to contemplate with pleasure."

While service *to* the people of God is an important aspect of our walk and calling, it really flows out of our response to God. Ministering to Him is our first priority. Because of who He is, His character, and what He's done, His redemptive work in our lives, we're free to trust Him, to take refuge in Him, as He places us in ministry.

Prayer: *O God, help me to serve you first and foremost. In Jesus' name. Amen.*

Thought for the Day: God's holiness is the only standard for living.

10
A CUE SHEET FOR LIFE

Psalm 14

The LORD looks down from heaven . . .
to see if there are any who understand, any who seek God.
—Ps. 14:2

I see reflections of Ps. 1 in today's reading. Who I listen to and take my cues from will color my relationship with God. They affect the direction of my focus when I approach Him in worship.

It's intriguing that the subheading under Ps. 14 in my Bible says "For the director of music. Of David." This could mean that the psalm was written for worship in the Temple, or maybe that it was intended to be spoken or led musically by the Levitical director of music.

But I just wonder if David had other intentions behind the phrase. I have no idea at what age David wrote this, but I suspect it was after he had attained an advanced level of maturity. I wonder if he glanced over at his well-worn harp and heard again in his mind some long-lost melody. I wonder if, on spying the stack of parchment manuscripts in the corner, he sang to himself a few of his creative masterpieces.

I wonder if all that prompted David to offer a little well-seasoned advice to a younger worship leader of Israel's congregation:

- Don't follow fads—follow God.
- Don't seek trends—seek God.
- Don't covet the opinion of others—covet God's blessing.
- Don't pray for people's approval—pray for God's anointing.

Wait a minute—I think he may be speaking to us!

Prayer: *Heavenly Father, beyond any style or format or trend or fad, I seek you. Above the approval of others, I long for the anointing of your Spirit. In your Son's name I pray. Amen.*

Thought for the Day: Styles change and opinions vary, but our God is eternal.

11

THE PRIVILEGE OF HIS PRESENCE

Psalm 15

LORD, who may dwell in your sanctuary?
Who may live on your holy hill?
—Ps. 15:1

In today's reading I couldn't get through the first two sentences without pausing to reflect on some subtle shadings in the text. What we read as "dwell" and "live" in verse 1 appears in many translations as "abide" and "dwell" respectively. All of these in the Hebrew indicate rest or recovery or lodging from a journey.

How appropriate for today! Who among us, in the middle of our culture's frantic pace, doesn't long for even a brief but oh-so-sweet respite in the dwelling place of the Almighty? Like the interior of a grand old cathedral along some busy downtown thoroughfare, His presence is a calm oasis in a land of arid activity.

But what a convicting set of requirements to approach God!

- righteous existence accompanied by a blameless walk;
- honest speech with no defamation of another;
- avoiding those who zap the life out of us and honoring those who are honorable;
- keeping a promise even when it's inconvenient, costly or painful.

What we read in Ps. 15 is also a good standard for just living. We don't see much in the way of these characteristics these days. I have to fully admit that I've failed miserably in these at times. You may recall that Jesus had a few things to say about approaching God with respect to those around us. (See Matt. 5:23-24.) His implication seems to be that even if someone has something against us, we need to get it right before offering ourselves to God. "Vertical" peace and "horizontal" discord can hardly coexist.

In verse 1, I find it quite significant that David asks, "Who may dwell in your sanctuary?" and "Who may live on your holy hill?" (emphasis added). He didn't ask who deserves to or who has the right to. It's as if he's acknowledging that no matter how well I get it here on earth, being in your presence, Lord, is still a privilege.

Prayer: *O God, perfect and holy Creator, I know full well that I don't deserve a moment in your presence. I know that the only good in me comes from and through you. Yet you desire to fellowship and even dwell with me. And for this I praise you with all my heart. In the name of Jesus I pray. Amen.*

Thought for the Day: Access to God is our privilege, not His duty.

12

ALL GOOD THINGS

Psalm 16

The boundary lines have fallen for me in pleasant places;
surely I have a delightful inheritance.

—Ps. 16:6

Looking around me, I can say with David that the boundary lines have fallen for me in pleasant places. Material blessings, financial security, job satisfaction, a stable family—all this is from God. I'm not wise enough to assemble the combination of elements that outline my life.

David said in verse 2 of this psalm, "You are my Lord; apart from you I have no good thing." This sentiment is echoed later in Ps. 107:8-9 as the writer exhorts the nation of Israel: "Let them give thanks to the LORD for his unfailing love and his wonderful deeds for men, for he satisfies the thirsty and fills the hungry with good things." I've come to realize that whatever "good things" surround me and whatever "good" is attributed to my life, it's only through and only because of God.

Regarding "delightful inheritance," or as the *New American Standard Bible* describes it, "My heritage is beautiful to me," not long ago a restaurant owner I did not know treated me with courtesy, respect, and honor far beyond normal protocol. It seems he recognized me by my name as being the son of a man he held in high esteem. This "Mephibosheth moment" was brought to me courtesy of my dad, a man for whom godly living was a definitive mark.

What are we doing to ensure this type of heritage for our future generations?

Prayer: *Father, you are the giver of good things, the bestower of blessings. May my life be marked by a grateful heart and a godly heritage. In your Son's name I pray. Amen.*

Thought for the Day: Everything in my life that is good, holy, and righteous comes from God.

13
APPLES AND SMILES

Psalm 17

Keep me as the apple of your eye;
hide me in the shadow of your wings.
—Ps. 17:8

Isn't it funny how certain phrases and colloquialisms become such a part of our everyday conversation that we hardly know where they come from, and we don't really grasp their original intent? That's the way I feel about this "apple of your eye" line. If you're like me, you've used it for a long time, and maybe, like me, for the longest time you didn't even know you were quoting God's Word!

I've always thought of "the apple of my eye" as being someone or some object that really holds my affection, that I cherish. And I suppose that's a part of the meaning behind this phrase. But the real intent, and what the original Hebrew phrase suggests, is the pupil of the eye. Of course, the pupil of the eye is a vital part of the optical organ and needs constant protection, covering, and meticulous care. It's also the part of the eye that allows light in and is the first receptor of the visual images around us. So care and protection of the pupil is essential to health. You can take a look at Deut. 32:10-12 for another, and maybe the first, use of this imagery.

While I'm extremely grateful for God's protection and care, as I'm sure you are, I really do relish the thought of holding God's affection, of being something He cherishes.

What joy and satisfaction there is in knowing God smiles on my life! Truth be told, I'm not always in that position. While I know for certain that God loves me just as I am—and too much to leave me there—I just imagine that He signs off on my day with pleasure when—

- I allow Him to vindicate me (v. 2);
- I keep my mouth in check (v. 3);

- I walk in His way, not mine (v. 5);
- He is my first thought, regardless of circumstances (v. 15).

Then I'll sense His protection, His shelter, and maybe, just maybe, His smile.

Prayer: *Loving Father, I long to be held as the apple of your eye—someone you protect, shelter, and shadow. I really do want my life to make you smile. In Jesus' name. Amen.*

Thought for the Day: Life's greatest pleasure is awakening to God's smile.

14
A DOXOLOGY OF PRAISE

Psalm 18

I will praise you among the nations,
O Lord; I will sing praises to your name
—Ps. 18:49

What a contemporary psalm is Ps. 18! Who can't relate? God is strength, rock, fortress, deliverer, shield, and stronghold, the only one who can redeem, rescue, and save.

Like David, I'm glad I don't get what I deserve according to my righteousness. I'm grateful that I'm seen through Christ Jesus. Since worship is a response to who God is and all He's done, we who have been forgiven much have much to respond to. In this psalm I hear echoes of Rev. 1:5—6: "To him who loves us and has freed us from our sins by his blood, and has made us to be a kingdom and priests to serve his God and Father—to him be glory and power for ever and ever!"

I'm sure David was cognizant of where he had been and what he was capable of. He had seen victory and defeat personally, morally, and nationally. Yet, he turns to God, recalling His deliverance in the past and claiming it for the future.

I love the fact that in the midst of recounting his troubles and numbering his enemies, David explodes into a doxology of praise. Oh, that I would be able to honestly do the same! "The Lord lives! Praise be to my Rock! Exalted be God my Savior!" (v. 46).

Prayer: *Lord, there are days when I'm certain that if you don't show up, I'm sunk. Be to me a rock, a fortress, a deliverer. Amen.*

Thought for the Day: A God who delivers is a God worthy of praise.

15

OUR MOST IMPORTANT THOUGHT

Psalm 19

May the words of my mouth and the meditation of my heart be pleasing in your sight, O LORD, my Rock and my Redeemer.
—Ps. 19:14

I've heard that there are more stars in the universe than there are grains of sand on every beach on earth. And every one of these celestial spotlights shines in praise of its Creator. As I look around me, I see every aspect of creation reflecting the glory of its Maker just by doing what it was designed to do. Oceans, mountains, weather patterns, animals—they all display infinite creativity and matchless imagination simply in being what they were created to be.

It's not difficult to see, really, and for the life of me I can't understand those who would attribute all this to chance. I'm thinking this is at the heart of Paul's discourse on "natural revelation" in Rom. 1:18-20. I can almost hear the natural world around me shouting, "Look at all this! It's because of God! It's all because of God!"

All this makes me cower in shame when I realize how pitifully short I've sometimes fallen in reflecting my Creator's glory. I'm afraid that on far too many occasions, my words, my thoughts, and my deeds have not truly honored God. Sometimes it has been presumptuous attitudes that have crept in, and at other times pride has sneaked in and sought to destroy relationships.

The good news is that God always offers us a way out of our human predicament. Read again verses 7-10, and take the time to absorb the benefits of His law, His statutes, His precepts, and His commands. In melding these into our lives, there is indeed great reward. Then our thoughts, our words, and our deeds overflow in ways that honor Him not only in our corporate worship gatherings but also in our daily, private living out of our response to our glorious Creator.

Prayer: *O Lord, so often my worship of you consists of trivial words accompanied by a selfish attitude. Refresh me again with the splendor of who you are and the glory of what you've done. I'm created for worship, and I want my words and my thoughts to please you. In Jesus' name. Amen.*

Thought for the Day: What we think about God is the most important thought we have.

16

TRUSTING A NAME, BELIEVING A PROMISE

Psalm 20

We trust in the name of the LORD our God.

—Ps. 20:7

There is protection and comfort and strength and power in God's name! The names He gave himself and revealed to us are tremendous reminders of His character, His essence, and His promises. To Abraham He was *El Shaddai,* God Almighty. To Isaiah He was the thrice-holy God. To David, a shepherd supplying all his needs. John the Baptist saw Him as the Lamb of God who takes away the sins of the world. Who is He to you?

Because we can trust His name, which describes His character, we can trust His promises:

Never will I leave you; never will I forsake you (Heb. 13:5).

Do not fear, for I am with you; do not be dismayed, for I am your God (Isa. 41:10).

"I know the plans I have for you," declares the LORD, "plans to prosper you and not to harm you, plans to give you hope and a future" (Jer. 29:11).

He has given us his very great and precious promises (2 Pet. 1:4).

Our God is a God who really wants the best for us. He's a God who will, if we'll submit, change our hearts and desires to become like His. And that's the point, isn't it? Our hearts like His. Beginning today, just now, let's make that our desire.

Prayer: *God Almighty, nothing is too hard for you, and no life is beyond your healing touch or rescuing hand. Change me today so that I see you for who you really are, as I trust in your great and certain promises. In the name of Christ I pray. Amen.*

Thought for the Day: By trusting God's name, we can believe His promises.

17

A FORMULA FOR PRAISE

Psalm 22

*You are enthroned as the Holy One;
you are the praise of Israel.*
—Ps. 22:3

Psalm 22 is viewed by most scholars as being "Messianic" in nature, and I'm sure they're right about that. After all, verse 1 was quoted by Christ on the Cross, and verses 7, 8, 14, and 16-18 all contain obvious foreshadowing of the suffering of our Savior. Still, I see in this psalm a formula for relief in times of our own suffering. In three steps, David lays out for us a pathway to healing and restoration.

Rejection (vv. 1-8): David openly and honestly acknowledges his situation, his I'm-up-a-creek-without-a-paddle season of life. If we're as honest as David, we can all admit to having been there to one degree or another: alone, alienated, betrayed, and—dare we say it?—forsaken by God. At least that's how it feels.

Remembrance (vv. 9-21): David's next step is looking back at his own history, retracing his life and seeing God's hand in it all the way. I'm learning to "remember" during my own troubling or trying times. I'm learning to recount the miraculous ways God delivered me in the past, even from my past. I want to lean, as David did, on the firm assurance of strong, everlasting arms.

Rejoicing (vv. 22, 25): Finally, strong in the strength of God himself and confident that God's deliverance in the past will be his in the future, David erupts in an acclamation of worship! "I will declare your name to my brothers; in the congregation I will praise you. . . . From you comes the theme of my praise in the great assembly." David's rejection called him to remembrance, which moved him to rejoicing.

In today's theme verse (v. 3), the phrase surrounding the word "praise" or "praises" has slightly different shadings according to which translation of the Bible you read. Among those shadings are "You are the praise of Israel" (NIV), "You who are enthroned upon the praises of Israel" (NASB), and "Thou that inhabitest the praises of Israel" (KJV). Despite the various wordings, I was encouraged when I discovered that the word we read as "praise" or "praises," as used here, in Hebrew is tehillah and indicates "a laudation" or "a hymn." I don't think it's a stretch to see this as adoration from a group, or songs and words of exaltation from a gathering of believers. I'm convinced that God brings His authority to bear on situations as His people—in a multitude of styles—worship Him.

Prayer: *O God, may our praise be such that it's comfortable for your royal presence and a delight for you to inhabit. After all, you are the theme. In Jesus' name. Amen.*

Thought for the Day: The Lord's rulership is realized wherever and whenever His people praise Him.

18

A MOMENT WITH THE SHEPHERD

Psalm 23

I will fear no evil, for you are with me;
your rod and your staff, they comfort me.
—Ps. 23:4

Sometimes it's difficult to see new things in a Scripture passage as familiar as this one. But, thank God, His Word never returns to Him void, and He's promised that if we seek Him, we'll find Him. So let's dig in.

I can't help but wonder what events in David's life led up to the composition of this incredible and universally loved psalm. In my Bible, the subtitle under the heading "Psalm 23" says simply, "A psalm of David." No historical backdrop, no cataclysmic event mentioned, not even a tune to accompany it—just "A psalm of David." Oh, that we would *all* experience whatever it was from the hand of God that prompted this steadfast statement of assurance!

The shepherd was a widely used metaphor in the ancient Middle East for earthly kings and especially for God. (See Ps. 28:9; Ps. 95:7; John 10:11; and 1 Pet. 5:4.) Yet David chooses here to use God's intimate, personal, covenant name, the LORD, *Yahweh*, to open this psalm. That sort of familiarity comes only from quiet moments in His presence and a heart open to His tender promptings.

The psalm continues with affirmations of a covenant relationship with the Almighty. It's reminiscent of the relationship between a king and a vassal: protection, restoration, guidance, and comfort. In picturesque language, David demonstrates how, in return for the King's watchfulness, he will bring honor to His name and move forth with confidence in his loving Father. Our shepherd/poet David surely had this in mind when he wrote in Ps. 56:3-4, "When

I am afraid, I will trust in you. In God, whose word I praise, in God I trust; I will not be afraid. What can mortal man do to me?"

I'm told that in the ancient world, treaties and covenants were often consummated with a celebratory feast and some physical sign of the agreement. A lavish table is depicted here, in the presence of David's enemies no less! His visible marker is a head anointed with oil and a cup overflowing with blessings. (See Rom. 15:13.) Goodness and love are sure signs that a covenant relationship has been entered into.

In this case, David assures us that it's personal and lasting: "And I will dwell in the house of the LORD forever" (v. 6). Knowing that we'll live forever with God, it's a wonder we get so hung up on temporal things.

Prayer: *O Lord, you are my shepherd and my king; you protect me, and yet you honor me; you feed me and you anoint me. Thank you that you are with me and that I'll be with you forever. In Christ's name. Amen.*

Thought for the Day: Personal time with God brings personal assurance from God.

19
A GRAND ENTRANCE

Psalm 24

Such is the generation of those who seek him,
who seek your face, O God of Jacob.
—Ps. 24:6

When we rid ourselves of idols, when we check the motives of our hearts and the actions of our hands, when we fully open up our spirits, then the King of Glory really does come in. And He comes to fight our battles, to conquer our strongholds, and to fill the space made for Him in our hearts.

I want to be a part of a generation who seeks God's face, and I want that legacy to be handed down to my sons and daughter. I long to be counted among those whose heritage it is to be God-seekers—those who live with the consuming passion to experience God face-to-face, dwelling in His presence forever. (See Ps. 23:6.)

It seems logical to me that whoever organized these psalms placed Ps. 24 immediately following reference to the house of the Lord, because it lays out for us who may aspire to the unique, awesome privilege of approaching God. The requirements?

- Clean hands (innocent actions)
- Pure hearts (selfless motives)
- No idol worship (nothing above God)
- No false swearing (honesty in speech and implication)

Make no mistake about it—this is a tall order! But when fleshly obsessions and distractions are put aside, there's room for the King of Glory to take His rightful place, to claim what's His to begin with, and to rule with authority over all the earth—especially over me.

Prayer: *Lord, I open my heart to you, I surrender my life, I lift my hands to you, I submit my desires to you. Reign in me. In your Son's name I pray. Amen.*

Thought for the Day: In God's kingdom, surrender leads to victory.

20

OUR TRUE FRIEND

Psalm 25

The LORD confides in those who fear him;
he makes his covenant known to them.

—Ps. 25:14

Earlier we looked at Ps. 23 through the lens of a covenant relationship. Today we'll take that one step further and see the joy that's ours when the covenant originator is also a friend.

They say the mark of a true friend is one who shares secret joys. I really do want God to be able to confide in me, to share with me, to reveal more of himself to me. One of the ways God has confided in me in recent days is through the incredibly intimate nature of His Word. He's revealed so much of His character to me by reminding me of His unchangeable attributes. He's shown me His ways; He's taught me His paths. He's guided me in truth, and He's become the source of my hope. He's become a friend with whom I can share my deepest longings and my most urgent needs. And—oh, yes—I've learned that He delights in my joys too!

In verse 15 of today's reading, David says, "My eyes are ever on the LORD," an echo of Ps. 141:8. Do you remember the story of King Jehoshaphat from Day 6? If you need to, refresh your memory by glancing through 2 Chron. 20 again. In verse 12 of that remarkable passage, we read the portion of Jehoshaphat's prayer that says, "We do not know what to do, but our eyes are upon you." If you're at all like me, you've got the "I don't know what to do" part down pat. It's the "our eyes are on you" line that gets me every time! Oh, that we could say with David, "My eyes are ever on the LORD."

There is confidence, though, in knowing that in God is the forgiveness, redemption, grace, and fullness of joy that David knows so well. One word of caution: Sometimes we rely on the Lord's pardon to such an extent that, if we're not careful, we begin to take it for granted. For David, that simply was not enough. In verse 21 he prays for integrity and uprightness, the enabling of a life lived as a reflection of He who is the ultimate good and the model of unmarred perfection. It's David's response to forgiveness. May it ever be ours as well.

Prayer: *Holy, perfect, and righteous Father, I want to be an image of you as I walk through this life. I pray that as we share our secret joys, my eyes will remain constantly on you, my only true and lasting friend. In Jesus' name I pray. Amen.*

Thought for the Day: Gaze on God's greatness; glance at the world's distractions.

INTEGRITY ISSUES

Psalm 26

Your love is ever before me,
and I walk continually in your truth.
—Ps. 26:3

Every now and then I get the unmistakable impression that I did or said something that was absolutely right and totally pure in motive. There are those times when my words or actions were not only appropriate but also exactly what was needed and called for. It doesn't occur as often as I would like, but occasionally it *does* happen! God help me to not become puffed up with pride at these times.

I'm convinced that David understood this, based on what I see in today's reading from Ps. 26. His appeal to God for an examination of his moral, spiritual, and relational integrity isn't so that those around him would be impressed. It's so that nothing would be standing between him and God. David wanted to be sure there were no obstacles that would hinder an open and honest relationship. David's plea for God to take notice of his innocence was so that he could "go about your altar, O LORD, proclaiming aloud your praise and telling of all your wonderful deeds" (vv. 6-7).

In other words, David longed for the freedom to simply do what he was created to do. And that can be our passionate pursuit also—to actually live our lives as the ones God himself described as "created for my glory . . . the people I formed for myself that they may proclaim my praise (Isa. 43:7, 21). Being comfortable with who we are in Christ and confident in what we're created to do in response is an absolute gift from God.

Prayer: Creator God, I offer my life to you today for your examination. I want nothing to stand between us and nothing to hinder my wholehearted response to you. Amen.

Thought for the Day: Created in God's image, we reflect His glory.

22
QUIET AND SECURE CONFIDENCE

Psalm 27

The LORD is my light and my salvation—whom shall I fear?
The LORD is the stronghold of my life—
of whom shall I be afraid?
—Ps. 27:1

The gifts we've been given—our talents and abilities—are not really where our strengths lie. Any of these could be taken from us in a moment. Or we could give in to our human nature and selfishly misuse them. Our real strength is in God. Why, then, don't we strive to know Him with the same passion we exhibit when we develop our gifts?

David seems to know exactly where his strength lay. Despite his victories, despite his accomplishments, despite his meteoric rise to fame, he saw all this as useless when faced with enemies attacking and armies besieging. What good is an impressive résumé when your spirit, your soul, your very life is threatened with annihilation? Ever been in *that* place?

The aggression required by the world we live in takes its toll on us. Competition in the workplace replaces the joy of simply doing a job we once loved. The lust for status leads us to spend greater and greater amounts of money on things we don't need and may not even particularly like. The overwhelming desire for wealth sucks us into the deceptive cult of those who believe we must have more, more, more.

And then tragedy strikes:

"You're fired."

"You'll need to file for bankruptcy."

"I'm afraid it's cancer."

"Mom, I think I'm pregnant."

"We have your son at the precinct now."

"This marriage is over!"

What now? What of our gifts, our talents, our abilities, our possessions? At times like these, the quiet confidence of Ps. 27 becomes our daily regimen.

Trust in Him (vv. 1-3).

Worship Him (vv. 4-6).

Ask Him (vv. 7-12).

Hope in Him (vv. 13-14).

Psalm 27 ends with a message that will be lost on us if we're not careful. Verse 14 says, "Wait for the LORD; be strong and take heart and wait for the LORD." We've all been taught the virtue of patiently tarrying, expecting God to act as we wait. However, the root word translated "wait" here is *qavah*, and it can mean "to bind together, perhaps by twisting." Imagine! Inextricably bound to God, our spirit "twisted together" with His. And that, my friend, is found when we're absorbed in His Word, not our world; when we're clothed in His righteousness, not our riches; when we rejoice in His Spirit, not our status.

That's real strength!

Prayer: *O Lord, more than wealth or riches or fame or fortune, I need you. You are serenity in a raging world and security in uncertain times. You are Jehovah Uzzi, the Lord my strength. In your Son's name I pray. Amen.*

Thought for the Day: Time spent waiting on God is never wasted.

23

TO SEE HIS HAND

Psalm 30

I will exalt you, O LORD,
for you lifted me out of the depths.
—Ps. 30:1

Moving into a new place of worship can be an exhilarating experience. Under the best of circumstances, it's a tangible sign that God is blessing a community of believers. It can be visible evidence that His people desire a venue to gather, extolling His name and proclaiming His wonders.

Psalm 30 was written by Israel's chief musician for the dedication of the Temple. Most likely, the occasion for this psalm is what we read in 1 Chron. 21—22. It beautifully portrays that worship is a response to God for all He is and for all He's done. When our congregations recall that even the highest heavens cannot contain God, then our cathedrals and sanctuaries, beautiful as they are, stand as monuments to His faithfulness and vehicles for His adoration.

Today's reading is an ideal follow-up to Ps. 29:1-2, where David implores his people: "Ascribe to the LORD, O mighty ones, ascribe to the LORD glory and strength. Ascribe to the LORD the glory due his name." We give God glory when we present an accurate picture or description of Him. One of the most powerful ways I know to present an accurate picture of God is by sharing what He's done in my life. He's been so faithful—a comforter, an encourager, a rescuer, and a redeemer.

I think that many times I've overlooked His faithful, gracious interaction in my life, and I've called it "coincidence" or "good luck." I'm learning, though, to see His hand more clearly. For a moment, think back on your own life. Has He rescued you? Encouraged you? Redeemed you? Then respond to Him with your whole heart! Exalt the Lord. Ascribe to Him the glory due His name.

An ancient prayer from the thirteenth century attributed to Richard of Chichester is a fitting conclusion to our meditation today:

> Day by day, dear Lord, of thee three things I pray:
> To see thee more clearly,
> Love thee more dearly,
> Follow thee more nearly,
> Day by day.

Prayer: God of Glory, mere words cannot capture your beauty. Nor can they express my thanks. You have redeemed me, and I am yours. I exalt you in the splendor of your holiness. In Jesus' name I pray. Amen.

Thought for the Day: A lifestyle of worship is a testimony to God's glory.

24
TRUTH, TRUST, AND TRYING

Psalm 31

Into your hands I commit my spirit; redeem me,
O LORD, the God of truth.
—Ps. 31:5

Someday when you've got the time, look in your Bible's concordance and track down all the times Jesus began a sentence with "I tell you the truth." Generally, these statements were followed by some astounding new insight or some seemingly contradictory statement. The point is, Jesus appears to have been saying, "Trust me on this one. I know what I'm talking about here."

Truth breeds trust. And that's what we're all seeking to hang our lives on. In this psalm, David calls God *El Emeth*—the God of Truth. The one we believe is the one we can trust. And in the one we trust we find refuge.

David employs the word "refuge" three times in this psalm as it's rendered in the *New International Version*. In verse 1 he speaks of taking refuge in God. In verse 2 he calls God "my rock of refuge" and in verse 4 simply "my refuge." The Hebrew word translated "refuge" implies "to flee for protection," but it also implies "to confide in; to put trust in." It's closely related to the word *batach*, the meaning of which extends to "being confident and sure" and even "to desist from labor."

How do you like that?—protection so secure, so worthy of our confidence that in falling into this refuge, we can cease striving and desist from laboring, letting Him be just what He said He would be. God as a Refuge is not an escape from reality. He *is* Reality.

Prayer: *O God, you are my rock, my refuge, my fortress, and my deliverer. Today I will run to you, I will rest in you, I will believe you. In Christ's name I pray. Amen.*

Thought for the Day: Trust Him, your truth. Rest in Him, your refuge.

25

YOUR OWN
SECOND CHANCE

Psalm 32

Blessed is he whose transgressions are forgiven,
whose sins are covered.
—Ps. 32:1

OK—let's face it. We've all been there. Some nagging sin eats away at our spirit, the memory of some past transgression robs us of today's joy, some powerful habit threatens to devour us as it mercilessly holds us captive. It could even be that the symptoms and results of this "sin-sickness" have actually caused some sort of physical malady. Strength is sapped, bones feel crushed, and our spiritual groaning never ends.

The precious five-year-old daughter of one of my best friends recently went through one of those rebellious and slightly defiant stages. When her daddy called her on her actions, he asked her why she thought she was behaving this way when she knew it was wrong. Heaven knows she had been taught better! With the forthrightness of a child, she responded, "Well, I guess because it's fun, and because you don't always catch me." Out of the mouths of babes!

Sin has a way of cruelly deceiving, doesn't it? We opt for instant gratification at the expense of long-term obedience. But sooner or later it catches up with us and the spiritual, emotional, and sometimes physical results are devastating. In all of this, is there a word from the Lord?

Well, in a word, it's *chesed*—divine relief. David discovered it when he could stand no more of himself and his sin. In desperation, he laid himself bare before God, and in return he received forgiveness and deliverance. Confession in his honest testimony led to "not guilty" as his verdict.

I think it's highly significant that David mentions both "transgressions" (*pesa*), which is rebellious, willful disobedience; and "sins" (*hata'ah*), which is sin in general. Both are forgiven, both are covered, both are washed away. The apostle Paul wrote, "In him [Christ] we have redemption through his blood, the forgiveness of sins, in accordance with the riches of God's grace that he lavished on us with all wisdom and understanding" (Eph. 1:7-8). Whenever we see "in accordance with" in the Scriptures, it means "according to" or "out of" or "in relation to." Just think—forgiveness "in relation to" God's grace. Just how far do you think that extends?

Think you've gone too far and God could never forgive you? God is all about second chances. Need proof? Just ask David. Ask Moses. Ask the woman at the well, or Paul or Peter.

Then ask Him for your very own second chance.

Prayer: *O Lord, your unfailing love is life to me. I come to you now relying on your mercy and your grace to cover me, to restore me, to deliver me. My hope and my trust are in you, my deliverer and my hiding place. In Jesus' name. Amen.*

Thought for the Day: The way out of bondage is found in His forgiveness.

26
AT HOME IN WORSHIP

Psalm 33

Sing to him a new song; play skillfully, and shout for joy.
—Ps. 33:3

Our natural state should be one of praising God. That's where we should be most comfortable, undeniably "at home." Unfortunately, for many of us worship is a little foreign and nowhere near second nature. Maybe we're distracted when we gather for worship with other believers. Maybe we have too much on our minds. We didn't prepare our hearts properly, or—here it comes—we just don't like the style.

Verse 1 of today's psalm says, "It is fitting for the upright to praise him." I like the way the *New American Standard Bible* puts it: "Praise is becoming to the upright." In other words, you're beautiful when you're worshiping God. If you were to look around you the next time your fellowship is engaged in worship, most likely you would see folks who have totally entered into the experience. You would notice that they're addressing God with their bodies, minds, hearts, and souls. You would notice that they're wonderfully comfortable. Praise is becoming to them. They're beautiful.

There are many references to "a new song" in the Psalms as well as in other books of the Bible. In addition to verse 3 in today's reading, Ps. 40:3; 96:1; 144:9; Isa. 42:10; and Rev. 5:9 all speak of this "new song." I've come to see that a new song as mentioned here is not so much concerning a style as it is responding to a fresh word from God, a generous outpouring of His Spirit, or a mighty move of His hand. You see, in each of the passages cited above, the new song celebrates God's saving act. Fearing God and enjoying Him don't have to be extreme opposites. His majestic power and holiness, plus His faithfulness and unfailing love, draw us to both responses.

Every mighty act of God among His people has resulted in fresh, new expressions in music. It's been that way throughout history. Do modern worship songs turn you off? Give thanks that God has moved significantly in the lives of those who have written them. Do traditional hymns bore you? Praise God that He moved the hearts and minds of those poets and composers as they wrote what were also at one time "new songs." Do sacred classics leave you cold? Be grateful that our creative God can be exalted in intricate rhythms and complex harmonies.

"New songs"—the result of our recognizing and acknowledging God's hand in our lives, responses to His salvation and deliverance.

A new song. Do you have one?

Prayer: *O God of perfection and creativity, place in me your new song. With all that I am, I want to praise you for all you've done. I want to be beautiful in your sight. In Jesus' name I pray. Amen.*

Thought for the Day: We are at home in worship when God inhabits our praise.

27
PRAYER AND PRAISE

Psalm 34

I will extol the LORD at all times;
his praise will always be on my lips.
—Ps. 34:1

"Extol" is not a word we use much these days, but I love the dignity and loftiness it implies. Some versions of our Bibles render the opening phrase of Ps. 34 something like "I will *bless* the LORD at all times" (KJV, emphasis added). When David wrote this, he used the Hebrew word *barak*, implying "to kneel, as in adoration." True worship always has physical implications.

Kneeling also leads us to consider the role of prayer in worship. God's Word is full of endorsements and encouragement where this is concerned. Need a reminder?

I pray also that the eyes of your heart may be enlightened in order that you may know the hope to which he has called you (Eph. 1:18).

Be joyful always; pray continually; give thanks in all circumstances (1 Thess. 5:16-18).

Do not be anxious about anything, but in everything, by prayer and petition, with thanksgiving, present your requests to God (Phil. 4:6).

I've begun to realize that the more I draw close to God, the more I begin to recognize His attentiveness toward me. What I'm really trying to do lately is just pay attention. I'm convinced God is working in and through my circumstances, and He's answering my prayers in ways beyond my wildest imagination. I just have to be alert.

Charles Wesley had it right in his magnificent hymn "Love Divine, All Loves Excelling":

> *Thee we would be always blessing,*
> *Serve Thee as Thy hosts above,*
> *Pray and praise Thee without ceasing,*
> *Glory in Thy perfect love.*

A Prayer for Today: *Father, today I will bless your name; I will extol you without ceasing. Help me see your hand in every circumstance. In your wonderful Son's name. Amen.*

Thought for the Day: Prayer and praise—both are needed.

28

IN THIS TOGETHER

Psalm 36

With you is the fountain of life;
in your light we see light.
—Ps. 36:9

It's true that when we think too highly of ourselves it affects our words and our treatment of others. We'll tend to use deceit to build ourselves up, attempting to impress those around us. This will eventually shape our thought patterns and our decision-making. It skews whatever wisdom we may have attained.

How different our lives are when we concentrate on God! Just as we noticed in Ps. 14, I tend to think that David may have wanted to be sure "the director of music" kept his ego in check and his self-image under control. Maybe he even wrote these words as a reminder to himself, Israel's most prominent and well-known worship leader.

Sometimes this is a challenge for up-front people in worship settings, isn't it? Ministries grow and gain a reputation not only for excitement but also for excellence. We begin to view that as a reflection of our own abilities. More and more people begin to comment on the theological depth of our speaking or the dynamic impact of our singing or the energy and emotion we bring to worship leading. And we start to believe it!

When that happens, we're walking on dangerous ground, friend. I can't count the number of times my father reminded me that none of us got to where we are in life all by ourselves. We ignore to our own detriment the teaching of those who influenced our upbringing. We fail to notice the contribution to Christ's Church that's being made by others, and we're headed for trouble. We see ourselves as God's greatest gift to His kingdom, and you can count on it—a fall is just around the corner.

David said in verse 2, "In his own eyes he flatters himself too much to detect or hate his sin." God help us when we ignore the contribution of others and inflate the importance of ourselves.

Prayer: *O God, how grateful I am for the teaching, instruction, and example of those who have gone before me! And thank you for the privilege of working alongside—not above or beneath—those you've placed in my world. In Christ's name I pray. Amen.*

Thought for the Day: Seeing the good in others leaves little room for flaunting the good in me.

29

NEVER FORSAKEN

Psalm 37

I was young and now I am old,
yet I have never seen the righteous forsaken.
—Ps. 37:25

Often when I pray about a situation or about a person who has crossed my path, I pray that the situation or the person will be changed. However, when I'm really in touch with God through my prayers, I discover I'm the one who is changed. As my desires and my needs become more focused in Him, I see my world differently, and I hope in a more godly manner.

A big-picture approach will define our day-to-day outlook. Remember what Peter wrote to the Early Church:

In this you greatly rejoice, though now for a little while you may have had to suffer grief in all kinds of trials. These have come so that your faith—of greater worth than gold, which perishes even though refined by fire—may be proved genuine and may result in praise, glory and honor when Jesus Christ is revealed (1 Pet. 1:6-7).

David lays out for us in Ps. 37 his own four-step program of recovery. Notice in verses three through seven that the focus is not on us but on God.

- Trust in the LORD (v. 3).
- Delight yourself in the LORD (v. 4).
- Commit your way to the LORD (v. 5).
- Be still before the LORD (v. 7).

I feel certain, too, that David passed this heritage of godly dependence on to his family. Look again at Prov. 3:5-6 and Prov. 16:3. Solomon, David's son and the author of these proverbs, certainly must have watched and listened to his father as he set out for us his own admonitions toward commitment and trust. It's all just good wisdom for living.

The most important thing we can pass on to our children is a legacy of faithfulness to and dependence on God. When I reach the final stages of my life, I really do want my children to see why I did the things I did. Whatever success I may have achieved in the world's eyes, I want that to pale beside a life that was spent following hard after God. It won't be a perfect life they'll see, but, God help me, they'll see that I was never forsaken.

Prayer: *Father, today I place all my trust in you, all my delight in you. I commit my way to you, and I'll be still so I can hear you. In Jesus' name I pray. Amen.*

Thought for the Day: A healthy fear of God and a total trust in Him lead to a successful life.

30
AN INVESTMENT PLAN

Psalm 39

Show me, O LORD, my life's end and the number of my days;
let me know how fleeting is my life.
—Ps. 39:4

I suppose all of us would like to know what lies ahead, what tomorrow will look like, and what next year will hold. I'm pretty sure, though, that if the future were to be revealed to us, we would probably be paralyzed by fear, discouragement, and anxiety.

If we really knew how long we were to be on this earth, what eternity is like, and how the two compare, I'm guessing that we would have a different take on "the real world." In fact, I'm certain our grip on the temporal would lighten as our anticipation for the eternal would heighten. But while we're here, it seems wise to pay attention to some precepts laid out for us in today's reading. I know that I, for one, must—

- Watch, or guard, my ways (v. 1). I need to set up a hedge or boundary around how I act, how I react, what I think, and where I go. This seems to apply also to the busyness of my life. More doesn't always equal *better*, and activity doesn't always mean achievement.

- Muzzle my mouth (v. 1). I don't think any of us need reminders here. How often I've wished for an "undo" button on my tongue! A quick trip through Prov. 10 is always a convicting but healthy excursion for me.

- Recognize life's brevity (v. 5). I heard a pastor say recently that most of us spend more time planning our summer vacation than we do preparing for eternity. That's a sobering thought.

- Acknowledge true wealth (v. 6). There are about a million ways to accumulate, invest, diversify, and distribute our financial gain. One of my dearest friends has said repeatedly that we should "do our givin' while we're livin' so we're knowin' where it's goin'." Still, it's only money, and we'll spend forever without a thought of it.

- Invest wisely (v. 7). The penalty for poor investments here on earth can hurt for a while, and that includes investments in money, time, and relationships. I want to spend my days investing in the things that truly matter—things that will last.

Mostly, I'm learning simply to *pay attention.* I'm beginning to notice how God moves in the everyday workings of my life. Big and small, they all matter to Him, and they should matter to me.

Prayer: *Lord, all the riches of the universe are yours, and you've given me a small portion to manage. Give me wisdom to invest wisely, to handle money properly, and to recognize what really counts. In Jesus' name I pray. Amen.*

Thought for the Day: Investing beyond this life pays eternal dividends.

31

AN ATTRACTIVE INVESTMENT

Psalm 40

I desire to do your will, O my God;
your law is within my heart.
—Ps. 40:8

Worshiping God and proclaiming His deeds really are attractive to people. Those we call "seekers" are by definition looking for something that's different from their day-to-day living. When they see a body of believers totally sold out in their worship of God, a mighty form of evangelism is taking place. Recounting the goodness of God—His work, not ours—intrigues people. It may initially draw them to us, but then our task is to point them to God.

In today's Scripture reading, I see several things that remind me of what we gleaned from Ps. 33. The concept of worship being attractive, especially to the seeker, really speaks to me. Those who join us for the first time are looking into the believability and relevance of Christianity, and their first exposure to it very likely will be in one of our corporate worship experiences. They're looking to invest their lives in something, and we don't invest our lives in things that are merely convenient. We invest our lives in things that cost us, but oh, are they worth it! Churches that make worship a priority understand the potential for outreach that it really has.

And remember that the "new song" we sing (v. 3), which is a response to God's amazing work in our lives, will have an effect. "Many will see and fear and put their trust in the LORD," David said (v. 3).

Who knows? Your participation in worship this week—your singing of a *new song*—may be the catalyst that drives someone to seek, to ask, to put his or her trust in God. Conversely, your lack of participation speaks volumes as well.

The centerpiece of Ps. 40 is verses 6-8, an expression of total surrender and obedience to God. Hebrews 10:5-10 applies these verses directly to Jesus himself, who while on earth gave us this insight:

> I tell you the truth, unless a kernel of wheat falls to the ground and dies, it remains only a single seed. But if it dies, it produces many seeds. The man who loves his life will lose it, while the man who hates his life in this world will keep it for eternal life (John 12:24-25).

Ultimately, spiritual acts of worship are presenting ourselves to God, allowing Him to transform us into His likeness, thereby pleasing Him. (See Rom. 12:1-2.)

Giving ourselves away is attractive to the world around us.

Say—how attractive are you feeling?

Prayer: *Father, may my life be one of total surrender to you. May my worship be an honest response to your mighty acts in my life. And may those around me see you, fear you, and put their trust in you. In your wonderful Son's name I pray. Amen.*

Thought for the Day: Offering ourselves to God allows Him to give himself to us.

32

WHEN YOU'RE DESPERATE

Psalm 42

Put your hope in God,
for I will yet praise him.
—Ps. 42:5

Desperation. Most of us have experienced it. If you haven't, you will. If you never find yourself in a state of desperation, you may never fully discover just how all-sufficient God is.

Most scholars consider Ps. 42 and Ps. 43 to have been one unit originally—a discouraged, anxiety-ridden plea of desperation. I have no idea what circumstances prompted the writer to pen these cries for help. Maybe there were armies surrounding him, some sort of national turmoil, or a fracture in his relationship with friends or family. Whatever the cause, we can be sure of one thing as old as history itself: when things get tough, it's not things we turn to.

I imagine that the writer of Ps. 42 was a leader in the religious activity of Israel (v. 4). I imagine that his undocumented question was *God, after all I've done in your service, this is how you treat me?*

Does that sound at all familiar? Whatever his attitude and whatever his circumstances may have been, this writer keenly senses his separation from God. He longs for that relationship to be restored—the joy of God's salvation, as Ps. 51 would put it.

When life is fractured, don't we all long for a solid, intimate reconnection with God? It's possible, you know. The answer is praise. He's brought you through before; He'll do it again.

Prayer: *O God, so often I'm desperate for you. At those times when I can't see your hand, feel your presence, or hear your voice, yet I will praise you. In Christ's name I pray. Amen.*

Thought for the Day: Our vertical relationship puts our horizontal situation in perspective.

33
EXCEEDING JOY

Psalm 43

Then will I go to the altar of God, to God,
my joy and my delight.
—Ps. 43:4

There's an ancient Hebrew reference to God known as *El Simchath Gili*—God, my Exceeding Joy. You'll sense the spirit of this name in Neh. 8:10, where this hero of the faith, Nehemiah, encourages his weary fellow workers with "Do not grieve, for the joy of the LORD is your strength."

I think deep down we're all searching for joy. We find joy when we discover purpose and meaning for our lives. We find joy in families that love and support us. We find joy in the fellowship of believers to whom we attach ourselves—living and working through this journey together. We find joy in fresh insight from God's Word and in seeing His hand in the daily workings of our lives.

But the writer of Ps. 43 is referring to something beyond simple joy. Actually, it's someone beyond mere joy. That someone is God, and He longs to be our exceeding joy.

For the longest time I've sort of passed right over the word "exceeding" when I read it in Scripture. We don't see the word so much in modern translations, but the King James Version records more than 50 uses of the word. Here are some samples:

Our light affliction, which is but for a moment, worketh for us a far more exceeding and eternal weight of glory (2 Cor. 9:17).

What is the exceeding greatness of his power us-ward who believe, according to the working of his mighty power (Eph. 1:19).

Whereby are given unto us exceeding great and precious promises (2 Pet. 1:4).

And my favorite:

> Now unto him that is able to do exceeding abundantly above all that we ask or think, according to the power that worketh in us (Eph. 3:20).

The point is, God's desire is not only to *do* and *give* more than we could ever imagine, but also to actually *be* for us and in us way beyond anything we could ever dream. That's not just joy—it's exceeding joy.

Prayer: *God, you are my exceeding joy. Far surpassing the temporal, you are my everlasting strength, my eternal defense, and my unending delight. In Jesus' name I pray. Amen.*

Thought for the Day: God exceeds our needs and outweighs our desires.

34

SILENCE AND STILLNESS

Psalm 46

Be still, and know that I am God;
I will be exalted among the nations,
I will be exalted in the earth.
—Ps. 46:10

God's might and power are sometimes best grasped when we're still. Being still may mean absorbing a breathtaking view of His creation or listening to His voice in a quiet place. At any rate, I know I'm not still nearly enough during the course of most days. But I'm learning.

It's during these times that spontaneous worship wells up within us. We can barely contain outbursts of thanksgiving, praise, and adoration. I think God delights in our heartfelt, unplanned, and unrehearsed moments of worship. A long walk on a starry night or a few quiet moments of solitude in a favorite spot at home can evoke deep responses in us. Even during a drive through the countryside, the interior of the car can become a sanctuary to focus on God and His handiwork. Don't try this one without practice, though—distraction from the road for too long may result in a "field trip" you hadn't counted on!

Yes, stillness and quietude are rarities in our world today. Time alone with God, listening to Him, and letting His Word wash over us are disciplines that, while difficult to establish in our daily routine, are absolutely essential for our growth and maturity.

I see something in this psalm, though, that reminds me that throughout Scripture we have many indications that corporate worship can be planned, its leaders can be rehearsed, and it can honor God. Actually, in the case of Ps. 46, that indication comes before verse 1. In my Bible, just under the chapter title I read "For the director of music. Of the Sons of Korath. According to *alamoth*. A song." While we don't know for certain exactly what each phrase means, it's not beyond the realm of good, biblical research to assume a few things:

This psalm was written either for Israel's choir director to add to his collection of liturgical hymns, for the choir director himself to lead, or for the choir to speak as they led the congregation in worship.

The Korahites were to have some part in this. They were descended from Levi and had definite liturgical duties, probably as a choir.

The Hebrew word for *alamoth* appears to mean "maidens." The phrase presented here may refer to maidens who accompanied the music with tambourines.

At least some portion of Ps. 46 was intended to be sung. That's what songs are for.

I'm a firm believer in allowing God to speak and move in our gatherings, but I also believe He can and does speak to us as we plan and rehearse for leading God's people into an awareness of His presence. Both are needed. Ps. 46 appears to be a case for the preparation of corporate worship, preparation that can take place only when we're listening to God—quiet and still.

Prayer: *God of Jacob, my Refuge, my Fortress, calm my spirit with an undeniable sense of your presence. Speak to me, Lord, as I quietly wait for you today. In Jesus' name I pray. Amen.*

Thought for the Day: Often, to hear God's thunderous voice we must be silent.

35
FAMILIAR WORDS

Psalm 47

God is the King of all the earth;
sing to him a psalm of praise.
—Ps. 47:7

Many years ago I discovered that choirs I directed really looked forward to the rehearsals when we didn't introduce any new music or spend any time being "nit-picky" about notes and rhythms and phrasing. We just sang.

The same is true from a worship leader's standpoint. Often those in our gatherings really appreciate the chance to sing what's familiar and well-loved. Not having to learn anything new, they open up like a wellspring from a heart overflowing from many honest and real experiences with their trustworthy God.

That's sort of how I view Ps. 47. Its themes are well-known, often repeated. It's familiar ground to us. Yet it has an excitement and fervor that's barely containable. Maybe that's why it was apparently used in ancient Jewish worship, most likely during the Feast of Tabernacles. And perhaps that's why it was later used in the liturgy surrounding the Jewish New Year festival, Rosh Hashanah.

After all, an affirmation and acclamation of God, "the great King over all the earth," would do us all some good. We know the words and the tune; they're written on our hearts.

What are we waiting on?

Prayer: *You, O Lord, are the great King over all the earth—and over my little world. I want my praise to you to be a comfortable, well-known thing. And I want my praise to be a comfortable habitation for you. In your Son's name I pray. Amen.*

Thought for the Day: The more I trust the sovereignty of heaven, the less I fear the calamities of earth.

36
ONLY WORDS?

Psalm 49

My mouth will speak words of wisdom;
the utterance from my heart will give understanding.
—Ps. 49:3

One of my sons e-mailed me recently asking for inspirational and challenging quotes to use for a specific project he was working on. It was really a lot of fun digging around, searching out gems of wisdom from people a lot smarter than me. What I discovered was that although I think I helped him in his project, I really helped myself. I uncovered some life-tested material, expressed in short, pithy terms that I can apply to my own existence.

For quite a while I've periodically concentrated on the Book of Proverbs. One chapter a day fills up a month and fills up my thoughts and speech. Every time I engage in this little discipline, I find myself applying the principles I read in the morning to some circumstance later in the day. It's uncanny! I always gain a more proper perspective on things such as prosperity or knowledge. And, yes, Solomon had a lot to say about—well, about what I say.

Have you ever been caught up in conversations that are at best trivial—at worst destructive? At the time they seem entertaining, maybe even important. But in the end they mean nothing—no life-giving words of encouragement, no soul-stirring word of support.

Maybe it's time we all reexamined the conversations we're having, the words we're using, and where all this information comes from. Maybe it's time that we, like the writer of Ps. 49, begin to intentionally speak words of wisdom—true wisdom—from the greatest treasury of wisdom we'll ever quote. After all, just as important as getting into the Word is being sure the Word gets into us.

Prayer: O God, Fill me today so that when I speak, others will hear you. In Jesus' name I pray. Amen.

Thought for the Day: There's no such thing as "only words."

37

THANKSGIVING AND THE HEART OF WORSHIP

Psalm 50

He who sacrifices thank offerings honors me.
—Ps. 50:23

Thanksgiving is powerful. When we thank someone, we affirm that person's worth and acknowledge a relationship. When we thank God, we affirm His worth, and we recognize who He is, who we are, and the relationship between us. I have a feeling that the sacrificial rituals Israel employed in their worship were never as important to God as the heart behind them.

Psalm 50 is attributed to Asaph, and we'll read more about him when we get to Ps. 73. We know now that "A psalm of Asaph" could mean that it was written by Asaph, written for Asaph, or written for the descendants of Asaph. At any rate, it appears that the psalm was composed for the liturgical worship carried on by God's people.

You may recall that King David had a worship ministry staff of sorts. In addition to Asaph, there was Heman and Jeduthun, and they were all descended from Levi, Israel's grandfather of the priesthood. The worship of God was a high priority in David's day, and each of these men seems to have had specific duties pertaining to worship. (See 1 Chron. 16.) Each of these men seems to have also had associates. You know, *someone* had to attend to the trumpets, the cymbals, and the incense!

I'm so grateful that God has blessed the music and worship ministries in some of our churches in such a way that one person simply can't handle the job alone. Several coworkers may be employed, and even then, volunteers are often needed to help fill out the ministry. Maybe you're in that position right now, or maybe not. It could be that during this particular season you're called to lead God's people pretty much on your own. If that's the case, I'm grateful for your dedicated commitment. I'm confident that God smiles not just on the size of one's ministry but also on the heart of one's offerings. Remember—it was God himself who said, "He who sacrifices thank offerings honors me, and he prepares the way so that I may show him the salvation of God" (v. 23).

Prayer: *Thank you, Father, for the blessings of life; for our churches' ministries, large and small; for the undeniable privilege of approaching you in worship; for the unspeakable gift of your salvation. In Jesus' name I pray. Amen.*

Thought for the Day: A spirit of gratitude inspires a heart of worship.

38

FAILURES INTO TRIUMPHS

Psalm 51

Restore to me the joy of your salvation.
—Ps. 51:12

So much has been written concerning Ps. 51 that I hesitate to add anything to what those with far greater insight and wisdom have already contributed. Then again, maybe so much has been written on Ps. 51 because so many of us identify with David's plea for forgiveness and restoration. There's absolutely nothing like restored joy, renewed fellowship, or the experience of God's unfailing love. The remembrance of my own sin should be grievous enough to keep me from going through that again. Yet I don't want that to keep me from celebrating God's grace and the joy of His salvation.

David's sin with Bathsheba is known well, as is his attempted cover-up that resulted in the murder of Uriah, Bathsheba's husband. Public disclosure of sin adds further stigma to an already crushed and broken spirit. However, alienation and shame seem to have driven David to first seek reconciliation with his God from whom he felt so distant. It's as if David couldn't bear to return to God's home until he returned to God's heart. In three stages David recognized his sin, recognized his sin's horribleness, and recognized that cleansing and restoration come only from God.

It's interesting that David should petition God to cleanse him with hyssop (v. 7). In Old Testament times, hyssop branches were used for ceremonial cleansing, particularly after death. Was David thinking of the death he instigated in the murder of Uriah? Was he referring to the child Bathsheba bore him who died within seven days? I tend to think that with the cleansing of hyssop, David was thinking of the death of an old way of life—a washing away of a former mode of living. I'm convinced he was longing for a brand-new start. In fact, when David says, "Create in me a clean heart, O God," the word he uses is *bara'*. It's the same word used for "created" in Gen. 1:27, and it means "from scratch" or "out of nothing."

It's something only God can do.

David's godly sorrow led to his true repentance. (See 2 Cor. 7:10.) This type of repentance leads to a life and spirit that God can renew and use in a mighty way. A broken spirit and a contrite heart are the kinds of sacrifices most pleasing to our Father. That's when He turns failures into triumphs and catastrophes into monuments of grace. Over and over the Scriptures ask the question "Is anything too hard for God?"

I don't think so.

Prayer: *O God, like David I cry out to you for mercy, for cleansing, for forgiveness, for restoring. May your steadfast love be my theme and your endless mercy my song. In Christ's name I pray. Amen.*

Thought for the Day: In God's hands tragedies become testimonies.

39

BURDENS BORNE DAILY

Psalm 55

Cast your cares on the LORD and he will sustain you.
—Ps. 55:22

It helps to read Ps. 55 in light of—or as a follow-up to—Ps. 53 and Ps. 54. Casting our cares on God might be seen as the overarching theme of this segment of Scripture. I know that casting my care on Him has become a frequent thing for me.

Like David, I know the sting of betrayal by a brother or sister, those I've worshiped with, those I've confided in, those I've shared large chunks of life with. When those sorts of relational fractures occur, extra grace is required all around. I know that without God invading my life, I, too, have the potential to be a betrayer. If I hope to be sustained, I'll cast my care on Him too.

Living as though God doesn't exist is just foolish. I love it when God works in some small yet undeniable way. And I'm grateful when I'm alert enough to take notice. Of course, I'm thrilled when He comes through in spectacular ways too! Most people turn to God, or at least acknowledge Him, when major trouble comes. But I'm learning that God wants to be involved in the non-catastrophic things also—to help, to soothe, to comfort, and to handle. When I really cast my care on Him, He takes charge of the situation.

In Ps. 68 David refers to God as the one who daily bears our burdens. Centuries later, Peter reminds us: "Cast all your anxiety on him because he cares for you" (1 Pet. 5:7). I suspect our loving Father knew we would need the reminder.

Prayer: *Lord, in the midst of darkness, I see you as light. In the midst of trial, I feel you as comfort. In the midst of suffering, I know you as healing. In Christ's name I pray. Amen.*

Thought for the Day: God's power takes over at our point of weakness.

40

WHAT ARE YOU KNOWN FOR?

Psalm 59

I will sing of your strength,
in the morning I will sing of your love.
—Ps. 59:16

A garment of praise is the remedy when we're wearing a spirit of heaviness. Praise turns our attention away from us and onto God. That's not an escape from reality—it *is* reality. You see, praise reminds us who we are and, better yet, who God is.

You're probably aware that I'm not the originator of this thought. Isaiah 61:3 speaks of the coming Christ, stating that He will provide "a garment of praise instead of a spirit of despair." And Neh. 8:10 assures us that "the joy of the LORD is your strength." I think it's noteworthy that it doesn't say the strength of the Lord is our joy.

We can all probably agree that the best songs ever written throughout history have been born of experience. No doubt, there's a measure of honesty and a depth of insight in them that we recognize and, in many cases, identify with. In my Bible, Ps. 59 states that it's to be sung to the tune "Do Not Destroy" and that David composed it when Saul sent men to watch his house in order to kill him. How's that for a day-lifter? I don't know about you, but I would be tempted to default into self-preservation mode. Left to my own devices, I would be likely to think of my own skin first.

But not David. He wasn't as interested in being known as a survivor as he was in being known for something else. There's a subtle difference in the meaning of "sing" as it appears in verse 17 and in the way it appears in verse 16. In verse 17, it implies "to celebrate in song and music." But earlier, in verse 16, the word is shiyr, or shuwr, and it depicts one who is "known as a singing man or woman"—not someone marked by difficulty but someone identified as a worshiper.

Prayer: *O God, my stronghold and my defense, whatever comes my way today, I choose to respond with singing, with praise, and with worship. Search me, and know me this hour. In Christ's name I pray. Amen.*

Thought for the Day: When trouble is known by us, what will we be known for?

41
YOUR TRUE HERITAGE

Psalm 61

*You have given me the heritage of those
who fear your name.*

—Ps. 61:5

I'm part of a heritage of worshipers. So are you. We don't do this alone. Every time we enter into a season of worship or prayer or reading of God's Word, it's not only as part of our local congregations but also with believers around the world who are approaching God.

In some mysterious way, our worship is linked to the millions who have gone before us. Many of those gave their very lives because they stood up and proclaimed their belief. In doing so, they serve as a pattern and encouragement to us. (See Heb. 11.)

Many churches include some sort of historic creed or affirmation of faith regularly in their worship. Many of these statements were formalized centuries ago, and if we can get beyond the mere words on a page, we'll see some pretty bold proclamations. Not only were these creeds and affirmations written to solidify doctrine—they were also often conceived at the risk of great persecution and tribulation.

I'm convinced that the world has heard enough of what the Church doesn't believe in. Please don't misunderstand: there *are* truths and practices we must live by. But as we've seen before, "seekers" are—well, seeking something. They want to know what we *do* believe in. They're looking for something to invest themselves in, something to hang their lives on, something that lasts.

Prayer: *Eternal Father, your truth endures, and your love is everlasting. I join today with all those who have gone before me in total worship. All the saints adore you. In Jesus' name I pray. Amen.*

Thought for the Day: An eternal God calls for enduring worship.

42

GOD ALONE

Psalm 62

Find rest, O my soul, in God alone; my hope comes from him.
—Ps. 62:5

God alone.

God alone.

God alone.

When will I ever learn? I wonder if David wrote Ps. 62 as an old man. He describes himself as a "leaning wall" and a "tottering fence" (v. 3). Maybe it was just the fatigue talking. It could be that the daily pressures of being a ruler coupled with international conflicts, added to myriad family concerns, were beginning to take a toll. Are you relating to any of this?

We're all boosted by the presence of hope, aren't we? Just the sliver of a promise for resolution or relief is sometimes all we need. I'm sure David felt that way quite often, but I'm really intrigued by his use of the phrase "my hope" in verse 5. Many times in Scripture "hope" is used to refer to a promise, and at times it refers to anxious expectation, as in waiting for something we're sure of. But here, David's use of "my hope" really indicates *a cord of attachment*. It was his lifeline! It's very similar to what Isaiah wrote in the familiar verse "Those who hope in [are attached to] the LORD will renew their strength" (Isa. 40:31).

Attached not to possessions or talents or relationships or status—but attached to God, God alone. That's a different kind of hope altogether!

Prayer: *Today, Lord, I'll attach myself to you—to you alone. My hope—my expectation—is in you. Speak, and I will listen. In your Son's name I pray. Amen.*

Thought for the Day: We draw strength and rest from what we attach ourselves to.

43

HEART POSTURE

Psalm 63

I will praise you as long as I live,
and in your name I will lift up my hands.
—Ps. 63:4

Our relationship to God is personal, emotional, and physical. No mere mental or intellectual acknowledgement will do here. We seek Him, we long for Him, and our bodies take on expressive gestures in worship. A relationship with God is total involvement.

The more I study David's life, the more I can mentally picture him in ecstatic worship—and in total depression. In either state, I can see his countenance rise or fall depending on his current proximity to God. I feel certain that David was keenly aware of the relationship between his spiritual state and his physical well-being. That's why he could say, "My soul thirsts for you, my body longs for you (v. 1). To David, his nearness to God was everything—spiritual, emotional, and physical.

We witness an increasing amount of discussion these days relating to the posture of worship. Do we sit? Do we stand? Should we kneel? Bow? Lift our hands? Remain motionless? When do we open our mouths? When do we close our eyes?

Today's highlighted verse says, "In your name I will lift up my hands." The Hebrew word used here is *yadah*. It comes from the root word for "hand" and in this form means "to worship with outstretched hands; to throw out the hands, especially in thanksgiving." See Ps. 141:2; Ps. 143:5-6; and 1 Tim. 2:8 for passages referring to the hands.

Shachad is another word with physical implications that is frequently translated "worship." In fact, it's used more than 80 times in the *New American Standard Bible* (NASB), and it literally means "to politely or respectfully bow; to bend low, to prostrate oneself."

Psalm 95:6 is one example of this gesture. To the ancient Hebrew, worship had deeply imbedded physical implications and dimensions.

Proskuneo is the principal New Testament (Greek) word translated "worship"—51 times in the NASB. It has lots of the same implications of submissiveness and respect yet includes the literal meaning of "a kiss toward." This obviously implies intimacy and closeness.

God's precious Word to us is full of gestural implications when it comes to worship. Ultimately, it's not our physical posture that really matters. It's the posture of our hearts.

Prayer: *O God, with my heart I adore you. With my lips I glorify you. With my hands I exalt you and salute your greatness. I am satisfied in you. In Jesus' name I pray. Amen.*

Thought for the Day: Loving God includes everything within us and everything about us.

44

TWO POWERFUL WORDS

Psalm 64

Let the righteous rejoice in the LORD
and take refuge in him.
—Ps. 64:10

God can handle our complaints (v. 1), and He's big enough to hear our worries and problems, even our doubts. An honest and open relationship with God will naturally include some honest and open dialog. I'm sure He's not at all thrown off or taken aback by our discontent. However, I get the strong feeling that He would prefer that we somehow move beyond our whining and trust Him with the results.

In verse 7 of today's psalm we see two very big and very powerful words: "But God." I understand that the words following this phrase in verses 7 and 8 are probably sentiments we're not too comfortable voicing today. David is referring to his enemies who conspire against him and would do him all sorts of physical and emotional harm. However, I'm encouraged by verse 9 and what David rightly sees as the result of fully trusting God, regardless of the dire circumstances he finds himself in: "All mankind will fear; they will proclaim the works of God and ponder what he has done." Even nonbelievers can see and acknowledge God's hand in the fruit-bearing life of a genuine believer.

"But God" is a phrase for even the most desperate and hopeless of situations. I'm pretty sure that's what Paul was thinking when he wrote to the church in Rome—and to us—about the most hopeless and desperate situation known to humanity, one in which we've all found ourselves: "But God demonstrates his own love for us in this: While we were still sinners, Christ died for us" (Rom. 5:8).

So the next time you're tempted to complain—and you will be, remember: God can handle it. Remember: He knows all about your situation. Remember: He wants to help. Remember: He *can* help. And remember two powerful words: "But God."

Prayer: *So often, Lord, I complain to you. I pour out my despair and my worries. Help me to remember you're there to comfort, to help, to protect. I will rejoice and take refuge in you. In your Son's name I pray. Amen.*

Thought for the Day: There are two powerful words for our too-challenging lives: "But God."

45

AN ENCOURAGING WORD

Psalm 66

Come and listen, all you who fear God; let me tell you what he has done for me.
—Ps. 66:16

Testimonies are powerful. But I'm afraid we're losing out on the impact they can have in our corporate worship settings. In our attempt to keep things centered on God—as they should be—we've shied away from articulating our personal experiences with God. But testimonies are ultimately about God, not us. You can see Israel's personal testimony by reading Ps. 136. Imagine it in a corporate setting with a priest leading and the people responding.

I can remember times in worship settings when a word was spoken about God's faithfulness. There was a young lady with cancer who told us she believed God could heal her. However, she said that if He chose not to, she got to be with Him. She pronounced herself a winner either way!

There was a fellow staff member whose wife had suffered two miscarriages. He told of that sorrow from his perspective. He assured us that God had told him they now had two babies in heaven.

When my wife, Vicki, lost all of her immediate family within just 13 months, she stood before our congregation and boldly proclaimed God's faithfulness. We needed that then, and we need it today.

Heb. 10:24 says that when we gather for worship, one of the things we're to do is encourage each other. I know of no better form of encouragement than reciting God's powerful work in our lives. Recalling God's faithfulness brings assurance to our future.

Prayer: *Father, as I recall your mighty work in my life, may others be encouraged as I tell of your faithfulness. In Christ's name I pray. Amen.*

Thought for the Day: Remembrance leads to praise.

46

A PLACE FOR YOU AND ME

Psalm 69

The LORD hears the needy and does not despise
his captive people.
—Ps. 69:33

There have been times when I've felt as if I needed God so desperately that all I could say was "Help!" To be quite honest, I still experience those times every now and then. How about you? Maybe it has nothing to do with calamity or disaster. Maybe it's just the lack of a fresh word that's choking us. Still, it's a feeling of desperation, isn't it?

In today's psalm, David wrote, "Save me, O God, for the waters have come up to my neck. I sink in the miry depths, where there is no foothold. I have come into the deep waters; the floods engulf me. I am worn out calling for help; my throat is parched" (vv. 1-3). He goes on to describe the tactics of his enemies who are out to get him, obviously much of the cause of his distress. But then a couple of lines shed light on one possible reason for David's suffering: "You know my folly, O God; my guilt is not hidden from you" (v. 5).

A self-inflicted wound. One of the great shames of the Church today is how quickly its people attack and then abandon those within the fellowship who have stumbled or completely fallen. While condoning or ignoring the actions of one who has fallen prey to the enemy's schemes is not the answer, there *is* room for loving discipline, accountability, and ultimately restoration. It takes some time, a fair amount of patience, and a lot of grace. Self-inflicted wounds are still wounds.

May those who hope in you not be disgraced because of me, O Lord . . . may those who seek you not be put to shame because of me (v. 6).

David knew full well the consequences and the potential consequences of his actions, his "folly," his sin. His worst fear was that he had brought shame and disgrace to those who feared God—a black eye and cause for embarrassment to his people, justification to forget that a flawed messenger does not negate the message.

In light of all this, I can't help but believe that the captive mentioned in today's key verse refers not only to someone held in physical bondage—a common scenario in David's day—but also, more importantly, to someone chained to the destructive influence of the evil one. These are the exiles of Jer. 24, and the one caught in sin we read about in Gal. 6. You may know one. You may be one.

If so, there's a place for you. It's a place above the deep waters and miry pits. It's a place beyond the taunts of your enemy and the accusations of your adversary.

It's a place called grace.

Prayer: *Gracious Father, what a perfect name for you! You are grace itself, a healing, loving place for me to run. Father, give me the grace not to withhold your love from a brother or sister who desperately needs it. In Jesus' name I pray. Amen.*

Thought for the Day: We may be the only army that shoots its wounded.

47

WISDOM FROM EXPERIENCE

Psalm 71

You have been my hope,
O Sovereign LORD, my confidence since my youth.
—Ps. 71:5

There's something beautiful about achieving longevity in one's walk with God. Dramatic late-life conversions are wonderful, and we thank God for them. But it's encouraging to see and hear from someone who has followed God since his or her youth and still lives out the Christian life.

I owe so much to those who have gone before me. I've been blessed with several mentors in my personal and my professional life. None of my mentors, and no one I would want to emulate, would claim to have arrived at their stations in life all on their own. It's a good thing for us to recognize and acknowledge the experience and wisdom of godly people who are older than we are.

Psalm 71 contains valuable insights into what seasoned citizens can declare through experience: confidence in God (v. 5); God, a strong refuge (v. 7); God's righteousness and salvation (v. 15); His marvelous deeds (v. 17); God's faithfulness (v. 22).

Newer is not always better, and younger is rarely wiser. Thank our Father for the godly influences in your life, and ask Him to make you a faithful mentor and advisor to those who follow. As Ps. 92 states, "The righteous will flourish like a palm tree. . . . They will still bear fruit in old age" (Ps. 92:12, 14).

Prayer: *Lord, thank you for godly saints who have modeled for me a faithful walk with you. Help me learn through them of your faithfulness. In your Son's name I pray. Amen.*

Thought for the Day: Age is a matter of the mind—if you don't mind, it doesn't matter.

48

AN UNHEALTHY COMPARISON

Psalm 73

My flesh and my heart may fail,
but God is the strength of my heart
and my portion forever.
—Ps. 73:26

A sense of entitlement leads to all kinds of resentment and envy. When I understand my calling, then I'm satisfied with my position and what God has provided. In fact, it's then I realize that God is really all I need.

I'm so glad the Bible includes the honest emotions and feelings of so many. Today we get to hear the heart of a contemporary of David, and maybe we'll see just a bit of a reflection of ourselves in his confession. Psalm 73 is attributed to Asaph, one of King David's choir directors. Perhaps he, like David, was an extremely accomplished musician, performer, and composer. And perhaps, like millions of those throughout history who have artistic temperaments, he was given to emotional extremes, high anxiety, a healthy sense of competition, and an unhealthy sense of pride.

Music, because of its performance element, can often be the foundation for comparison, envy, and jealousy. And because it tends to bypass the intellect and go straight for our emotions, music has an incredible power over its listeners, its composers, and its performers. As a musician myself, I can say with confidence and authority that we even compare ourselves with ourselves, as we try to outdo what we perceive as our greatest accomplishments.

Asaph seems to have been prone to all of the above. He said, "But as for me, my feet had almost slipped; I had nearly lost my foothold. For I envied the arrogant when I saw the prosperity of the wicked" (vv. 2-3). How's that for an open confession? Like many of us do, he began to see those around him as living perfect, carefree lives:

They are without struggles (v. 4).

They are healthy and strong (v. 4.)

They have no burdens (v. 5).

They have no sickness (v. 5).

And in a resentful retort, he adds—

They're prideful (v. 6).

They have callous hearts (v. 7).

They speak with malice (v. 8).

Asaph's pity party continues as he compares himself—self-righteously—with those around him whom he sees as being much better off. In verses 13 and 14, he laments his faithful living and his meager existence. And then God—as only God can—reminds Brother Asaph of what security is and what it isn't; of what a foundation is and what a folly is; of what is ephemeral and what is eternal.

Coming to his senses, Asaph responds, "Whom have I in heaven but you? And earth has nothing I desire besides you. . . . God is the strength of my heart and my portion forever" (vv. 25-26).

And with that, nothing compares!

Prayer: *O God, today remind me that nothing is greater than your provision, and nothing satisfies like your love. Give me your calm assurance that I am perfectly in your will, in your control, in your time. In Jesus' name I pray. Amen.*

Thought for the Day: The protection of God is all the provision we need.

49

FOR GOD AND COUNTRY

Psalm 76

He breaks the spirit of rulers;
he is feared by the kings of the earth.
—Ps. 76:12

Sometimes I struggle with how to balance my faith and my Christian convictions with my civic responsibilities and allegiance. This may be especially troublesome for those of us who are charged with leadership roles in worship settings. How do we appropriately express our patriotism without giving the impression that our ultimate trust is in our government rather than in our God?

Patriotic-themed events have been popular in our churches for a while now, and current situations around the world surely make us want to stand up, salute the flag, and wrap ourselves in red, white, and blue. I love my country, the United States. There's no place I would rather live. I'm a firm believer in the fundamental principles that have made our nation the greatest on earth. But this psalm helps me see how God can be honored *because of His work* in our land.

I get the impression that David and Asaph—probably the writers of Ps. 76—saw little if any disparity between love of God and love of country. In what has been claimed to be the last recorded words of David, he stated, "When one rules over men in righteousness, when he rules in the fear of God, he is like the light of morning at sunrise on a cloudless morning, like the brightness after rain that brings grass from the earth" (2 Sam. 23:3-4). In other words, there's a freshness and a life-giving quality to the leadership of those who govern with the precepts of the Almighty in the forefront.

We in response are called to submit ourselves to the authority of those whom God has placed over us, even when—and here's the catch—they weren't who we voted for! Paul's discourse in Rom. 13

is a good example for us. I can't imagine a more oppressive atmosphere politically than the one he was experiencing when he wrote this. Still, the call for subjection and respect is there. And it's for us, as well as those first-century believers, since God has placed us in this time and in this place. Of course, there are rare instances in which we have to stand firm in the tenets of our faith when they are opposed to some sort of government legislation. But be assured of this: God may move behind the scenes, but He moves all the scenes He's behind.

Prayer: *God of our Fathers, in wisdom and righteousness you ordained our nation. Help us remember that our only hope for the future is in you. In Jesus' name I pray. Amen.*

Thought for the Day: Love for God and love for country need not be mutually exclusive.

50

ANCIENT INSIGHT FOR TODAY

Psalm 78

I will open my mouth in parables, I will utter hidden things, things from of old—
what we have heard and known, what our fathers have told us.

—Ps. 78:2-3

We have a responsibility to hand to our children the faith we cherish. They must make it their own, of course, but nurturing them in the ways of God is essential.

Asaph, the writer of Ps. 78, was well acquainted with this concept. I feel certain he was familiar with Deut. 6 and its outline for a secure home. Known as the *shema*, Hebrew for "hear," as in verse 4, this chapter from the fifth book of the Bible was burned into the souls of Jewish families for thousands of years:

Hear, O Israel: The LORD our God, the LORD is one. Love the LORD your God with all your heart and with all your soul and with all your strength. These commandments that I give you today are to be upon your hearts. Impress them on your children. Talk about them when you sit at home and when you walk along the road, when you lie down and when you get up. Tie them as symbols on your hands and bind them on your foreheads. Write them on the doorframes of your houses and on your gates (Deut. 6:4-9).

Will our children see in us lives distinguished by an allegiance to the Word of God? Will they hear an undeniable affirmation of the faithfulness of God? The responsibility is ours, and so is the privilege.

Prayer: *Father—what assurance and joy it is to call you by that name! May your words, etched on my heart, spill from my tongue as I reflect you. In Christ's name I pray. Amen.*

Thought for the Day: As we apply ourselves wholly to God's truth, we apply God's truth wholly to ourselves.

51
A REASON TO CELEBRATE

Psalm 81

Sing for joy to God our strength;
shout aloud to the God of Jacob!
—Ps. 81:1

Praising God with music was a decree and a mandate for ancient Israel. Can it be any less for us? In a culture in which we're surrounded by others who speak languages we don't always understand, the language of praise should fit us comfortably wherever we are.

I'm convinced that we don't celebrate enough. We host parties and attend observances, but rarely do we participate in a no-holds-barred celebration. And of all people, we have something to celebrate—redemption, salvation, and an eternal home! I'm afraid that too many shallow things pass for celebration these days, so that when the real opportunity arises, we don't always know what to do with it.

Maybe that's why God commanded the people of Israel to celebrate. They were to mark significant events with unbridled celebration. Ps. 81 is what scholars call a "festival song." It's a musical memorial to *Elohi Mauzi*, "God our Strength." Most likely, it was composed for ceremonies surrounding a new year—the New Moon, in Asaph's terminology—or the beginning of the Feast of Tabernacles, or, as it was often simply called, The Feast. The point is, God ordained and established celebration as a statute.

It's appropriate that the change of seasons be accompanied by festivities. New seasons remind us of where we've been, and they celebrate the anticipation of what lies ahead. When you think about it, most holidays offer a little bit of both. We look back with gratitude—or regret—and we look ahead with hope—or perhaps, trepidation.

The same is true with the seasons of life. We all live in them, but do we celebrate them? I suppose there are times for each of us when we enter a new season of life, and we don't feel much like celebrating. Perhaps we were forced into it through a set of ugly circumstances. Maybe the loss of a spouse, family member, or friend has brought us to our own "New Moon." Our jobs are eliminated, or our health is depleted, and the last thing we want to do is party. Yet in those times in my life, I hear God reminding me of what He's brought me through and His promise to be with me in the days to come. He tends the wounds of my yesterday with the balm of His tomorrow.

And the scars? They remind me that healing has taken place at the hand of a mighty rescuer. So I'll celebrate.

Prayer: *O God my strength, because of all you've done in my life, I'll celebrate your goodness, your mercy, your abundance. I'll sing, I'll shout, and I'll play music to your name. But Lord, help me always remember why. In Jesus' name I pray. Amen.*

Thought for the Day: Never hesitate to celebrate a God who's great.

52
A WORD ON THE WORSHIP WARS

Psalm 83

Let them know that you, whose name is the LORD—
that you alone are the Most High over all the earth.
—Ps. 83:18

It's easy to assume that "our way" is "God's way." If others don't agree with us, then they're obviously less spiritual than we are. In our current day and age, there may be no place that this is more evident than in the issue of worship style.

I may have just touched a sensitive nerve here, but it's worth thinking about. Most of the battles in our current—and dreadfully unfortunate—worship wars revolve around music, more particularly around musical style. Rarely in these skirmishes are we upset over theological issues, the authority of Scripture, or the deity of Christ. It's not *what* we say so much as it is *how* we say it.

Here's a little quiz. Ask yourself—
- What kind of music does God like?
- What's His preferred order of worship?
- Is He partial to stained glass over theatrical lighting?
- Is He into projected lyrics rather than hardback hymnals?

We chuckle at questions like these, but don't we all get caught up sometimes in worship-related issues that are just as trivial? We disdain the "superficiality" of modern worship songs with no regard for the fresh expression they bring. We dread the "boredom" of classic hymns and forget the theological depth they bring to our understanding. And regardless of which "camp" we support, the use of any musical instrument that's not within our accepted arsenal is seen as suspect in its godliness. We ignore the fact that dozens of musical instruments are listed in Scripture.

The truth is, our way is often not God's way. And I'm pretty sure that God's not even concerned with what our way is. In the end, it's not about us anyway. It's about Him. It's not about what we get out of worship—it's about what we *give*. It's not about whether our needs are met—it's about whether His name is exalted.

Prayer: *Most high God, forgive me when I've placed my desires and wants above your name and majesty. What I give in worship really is all about you. In the name of your wonderful Son I pray. Amen.*

Thought for the Day: God is above any style, any preference, any tradition.

53

PROVISION, POSITION, AND POWER

Psalm 86

Teach me your way, O LORD, and I will walk in your truth;
give me an undivided heart, that I may fear your name.
—Ps. 86:11

Even believers can put God in second or third place in their hearts. It's easy to see this in others, and sadly, it's easy to point out. But this sort of misplacing of God can be deceptive when it's our own situation, our own lives.

We face today an unprecedented opportunity for media and information overload. Our senses and our intellect are bombarded, even assaulted, on a daily basis. Just keeping our focus can be a daunting task. True, some of what confronts us is good, yet it can still be a distraction from what's best.

I don't know exactly what caused David to plea for an undivided heart, but I have my suspicions. Some things never change, and they're as old as humanity itself. A longing for security is universal. A sense of purpose has been a desire of humans from the beginning of time. And pride, the source of all our sin, has infiltrated the soul of everyone who has ever drawn a breath. In our efforts to address each of these, we often exhaust every last ounce of strength within us in our attempts to make ourselves look good, to promote our own abilities, to appear perfect—as if we really could.

Thankfully, we have a solid outline in Ps. 86 that can help us put things, and especially God, in proper perspective. In verses 1-7 David speaks of God's provision. Verses 8-10 refer to God's position. And in verses 11-16 we see God's power.

By the way, the word "teach" in verse 11 is *yara*, and one of its meanings is "throw or shoot as an arrow." Amazing, isn't it? The arrows of God's truth don't injure our hearts—they heal them.

Prayer: *O God, I place you above all my desires, all my ambitions, all my longings, all my wishes, and all my plans. So that I may honor you, give me an undivided heart. In Jesus' name I pray. Amen.*

Thought for the Day: An undivided heart leads to an uncontested allegiance.

54
ETHAN'S POINT

Psalm 89

Blessed are those who have learned to acclaim you.
—Ps. 89:15

Those who look God-ward in all of life's experiences see the world from a different perspective than those who do not. Because I long for that sort of perspective, I've asked God recently to "increase my capacity" for Him—to see the world and other people as He sees them, to get a grip on what it is He's trying to teach me, to simply be more God-conscious.

Ethan, the composer of Ps. 89, was probably the same person as Jeduthun, the associate of Asaph and Heman whom we met earlier. If you remember, these men were primary leaders in King David's worship ministry staff. If you want the full roster, take a look at 1 Chron. 6, but don't ask me for help in pronouncing all those names!

Ethan was apparently a descendant of Levi, about 13 generations removed. Given the oral tradition of Israel and the lifespan of human beings in that day, it's likely that he heard many accounts of God's miraculous work among His chosen people. The calling of Moses, the series of plagues on Egypt, the Exodus, the parting of the Red Sea, God's care and protection while they wandered in the wilderness—this grand litany of liberation must have sounded so tangible to him that it was as if he had lived through it himself.

So Ethan writes, "With my mouth I will make your faithfulness known through all generations" (v. 1). I love the way the *New American Standard Bible* renders today's key verse: "How blessed are the people who know the joyful sound!" (v. 15). Yes, remembering, sharing, and celebrating God's work in the past is a glorious and needed thing. But I'm sensing that God wants me to notice Him right here, right now. I want to walk through today taking notice of the evidence that surrounds me of His participation in my life.

95

I've discovered that when I'm searching for Him, I find Him. When I'm on the lookout for His hand, I see His fingerprints everywhere. When my thoughts, words, actions and reactions are filtered through Him, the things that are detrimental distractions to me seem to fade away.

Maybe that's the point Ethan was trying to make.

Prayer: *God of yesterday and today, increase my capacity for you. As I recognize your work in the past, help me see the wonder of you in the present. In Christ's name I pray. Amen.*

Thought for the Day: Yesterday and today—they're all His.

55
OUR SECURITY SYSTEM

Psalm 90

Teach us to number our days aright, that we may gain a heart of wisdom.
—Ps. 90:12

Who knows how long his or her life will be? Every day is a gift to be used and used up. Responding to God in a right way makes our days and our work fulfilling. He gives purpose to both. A God of eternity can surely handle managing my short life.

Moses, the author of Ps. 90, certainly understood the importance of a dwelling place. More accurately, he knew the significance of a lack of permanent housing! You may recall that he was in the driver's seat when he led about two million of his closest friends on an extended family vacation—40 years of wandering on a trek that could have been accomplished in about two weeks. But, oh, what lessons the Israelites learned on their seemingly aimless sojourn—lessons such as trusting God, trusting God, and trusting God!

Have you ever felt like a wanderer? Have you ever felt that life, especially *your* life, was directionless, going nowhere? And in all of that, did you feel as if God were just completely silent and that He had totally abandoned you?

You'll recall that the Israelites often felt like that as they meandered in the wilderness, grumbling against Moses and ultimately against God himself. I can't imagine the frustration God must have felt toward them as He lovingly reassured them of His presence and His protection, even as He was forced on occasion to chastise and discipline them. And I can't imagine the frustration God must feel toward me when I steadfastly refuse to listen to Him and set out on my own course—only to wind up feeling just as directionless as Moses and Company.

I don't really know if Moses wrote the words we read in Deut. 33:27 before or after he wrote this psalm, but the sentiment is the same: *The eternal God is your refuge, and underneath are the everlasting arms.*

Somewhere amid all the doubts and questions and complaints, Moses learned that temporal surroundings really offer a false sense of security. Here today, gone tomorrow. Only our relationship to the everlasting God—who formed and sustains the universe, and for whom time is nothing—only that relationship will last. Only that security is of any true significance.

Prayer: *Eternal Father, my life is in your hands, my future in your keeping. May all my days and the work that fills them up reflect a trust in you that far outweighs my doubt and confusion. In Jesus' name I pray. Amen.*

Prayer: God is big enough to handle our questions, and He is compassionate enough to love us through them.

56

YOUR DWELLING
PLACE OF CHOICE

Psalm 91

He who dwells in the shelter of the Most High
will rest in the shadow of the Almighty.
—Ps. 91:1

Psalm 91 is a good complement to yesterday's reading, Ps. 90. We have to *choose* our dwelling place, you know. We must decide with whom we will identify. "To dwell with" seems to indicate an investing of myself. I have to make that choice carefully and confidently.

What is it that frightens you most? What is it that fills you with dread down to your very soul? Does it pertain to your health? Your job? Your reputation? Your family? What is it that, if removed from you, would shake you to the core? What attack could you sustain that would cause you to question your faith, even your faith in God?

Psalm 91 is ascribed to no author, but I imagine it was written by someone with liturgical duties in the Temple and was used, at least in part, as an encouragement to the worshipers. And that's what we are to do also. (See Heb. 10:24.) When we gather for worship, a word of encouragement, support, or testimony is needed. Telling others what God has done in my life can be incredibly edifying and life-giving. I shudder to think how many times I've missed that opportunity by replacing it with trivial talk and negative conversation.

The psalmist here will have no part of that. Instead, he acclaims the power of God and His interaction in our lives. And he gets fairly specific. In verse 3 he states, "Surely he will save you from the fowler's snare and from the deadly pestilence." While the snare and pestilence may be metaphoric language, his use of the word "save" is not. In fact, the Hebrew word—often translated "refuge"—used there is *natsal*, and it means "to snatch away, to pluck, to take out." I marvel at God's goodness in my life when, despite my ignorance or my obstinacy, He's plucked me right out of a situation or relationship that could be potentially dangerous. There may be someone today who desperately needs to hear of God's saving grace in your life. Specifics are probably not needed, but a word of encouragement to the hopeless might be the lifeline they need when they're sinking in the stuff of life.

At the end of the day, we're all in the same boat—travelers in need of a shelter and a hiding place. We can't lift each other up if we're tearing each other down.

Prayer: *O Lord, so many times you've rescued me when despair was trying to sink me. Give me courage to claim you as my refuge and my fortress so that others will see and have hope. In the name of Christ our Savior I pray. Amen.*

Thought for the Day: Dwelling in His shelter means resting in His shadow.

57

FIRMLY PLANTED

Psalm 92

They will still bear fruit in old age,
they will stay fresh and green.
—Ps. 92:14

Today's psalm is subtitled as one for the Sabbath—a day of worship, rest, and reflection, a day to acknowledge God and sing for joy at the works of His hand (v. 4). No doubt about it: a little time taken to rest and reflect is not only a good idea, it's also God's idea.

Growing in the faith and being nurtured by the Word takes time. And it takes a good, solid, and proper setting. I'll be forever grateful for the godly heritage my parents have left me and for the strong, biblical teaching I've been exposed to in churches I've been associated with. I don't know about you, but for me, growing in my walk with the Lord requires me to expose myself to good teaching and allow it time to be absorbed into my spirit before I can fully apply it to my life. Sometimes personal reflection in a period of rest is the only way I can be sure this is accomplished.

The righteous will flourish like a palm tree, they will grow like a cedar of Lebanon; planted in the house of the LORD, they will flourish in the courts of our God. They will still bear fruit in old age, they will stay fresh and green (vv. 12–14).

I'm no master gardener, but I do love working in my yard. In fact, if a few days go by without getting my hands dirty, I get a little uptight. There's nothing quite like working up the soil, watching things grow, and beholding the incredible beauty and variety God has infused into plant life. By the way, there's nothing quite as exciting, at least for me, as the day the new seed catalogs begin to arrive in the mail!

One thing I've learned the hard way is that the seeds I plant must be placed in a proper setting—the right kind of soil, the right amount of sun or shade—and they must be fed, watered, and pruned accordingly. My zinnias require surroundings different from my hostas. My crepe myrtles will do better if I don't treat them like dogwoods.

If I'm going to flourish, stay fresh and green, and bear fruit in my old age, I have to be firmly and correctly planted too. I need room to grow where I'll be fed and nurtured in the right surroundings. I need to be tended, and sometimes pruned, in the way that best enhances my survival—planted, as today's psalm says, in the house of the Lord.

Prayer: *O God, the beauty and wonder of your creation makes me bow in absolute wonder. May I never stop being in awe of your attention to all you've made and your constant care for me. In Christ's name I pray. Amen.*

Thought for the Day: We bloom best when we're correctly planted.

58
DON'T FORGET TO REMEMBER

Psalm 95

Come, let us bow down in worship,
let us kneel before the LORD our Maker.
—Ps. 95:6

My worship of God must be an investment of all that's in me. As we've noted before, there are physical gestures related to worship, and today's psalm calls me to sing for joy, shout aloud, extol him with music, bow down in worship, and kneel before Him. But worship is much more than my physical posture.

I see Ps. 95 as a call to worship, and it's not hard for me to imagine a priest standing before the Israelites, imploring them with these words as they entered the Temple area. Preparation for worship is a vital thing. How often I've entered into a season of worship with little or no preparation of my heart and spirit! All too often I come away from such gatherings feeling empty, as if I've simply gone through the motions.

If, on the other hand, I've prepared my heart and spirit before entering such a time, I find that my worship really is a response to Him, not something I have to generate. And for me, "remembering" is a prime motivating factor:

- I remember that there is one God who alone is worthy of my adoration (vv. 3-5).
- I remember that sovereignty is God's alone. Why would I even want to assume authority over my own life? (vv. 6-7).
- I remember all that He's brought me through and that He's more than capable of seeing me through today (vv.7-9).
- I remember that unbelief—simply not taking God at His word—has been a major stumbling block for me (v. 10).

When I forget God's powerful, restorative work in my life, then anxiety and worry fill my days. When I remember that there is one God, even though our culture screams for allegiance to many lesser gods, then I feel prepared—though quite unworthy—to approach Him, not with a hardened, callous heart but with a spirit of gratitude that He has called me, a wayward child, into His arms—the arms of a loving Father.

Prayer: *God, my Maker, when my heart is cold and forgetful, remind me of who you are and what you've done. Melt my disbelief with assurance of your total control in my life. Whatever I face today, help me remember you. In your Son's name I pray. Amen.*

Thought for the Day: More than the bending of knees, God searches for the bowing of hearts.

59

A WORD FROM JOB

Psalm 97

The heavens proclaim his righteousness,
and all the peoples see his glory.
—Ps. 97:6

You've probably seen it before. We gather for worship, and in our attempt to make our meeting relevant, welcoming, and comfortable, we lose sight of who God really is. We know He wants us to approach him (Heb. 4:16), and we consider Him a friend who sticks closer than a brother (Prov. 18:24). But He is, after all, the sovereign Creator of the universe, the King of Kings, the Redeemer of the world, and the Savior of our souls.

When we begin to see God for who He really is, we gain an entirely new way of looking at the world around us. We often sing about our desire to see God, to touch Him, or to experience Him fully. And those are noble desires. But I have to wonder: *are we really ready for that?*

I know you remember the saga of Job, how he was subject to all kinds of disasters through no fault and with no understanding of his own. I'm sure you recall how his "support group" droned on and on, philosophizing about his pitiful condition. I wonder if, in his sad state, Job might have felt just the slightest bit uppity, considering how he, the righteous and blameless servant of God, had been treated so unfairly and judgmentally condemned by his peers. Maybe he considered himself one of those who suffered for the Lord—and a little bit proud to have this "honor" bestowed on him. This is total speculation on my part, but I *do* know that he began to ask where God was in all this.

Then God spoke. Thunderously, authoritatively, and majestically—God spoke.

Job's response?

My ears had heard of you but now my eyes have seen you. Therefore I despise myself and repent in dust and ashes (Job 42:5-6).

Indeed, our worship gatherings need to be welcoming, relevant to our world, and friendly. But we must remember exactly who we're addressing here.

And when He speaks, hold on.

Prayer: *Creator God, I, too, long to see you, to touch you, to feel your presence. Shake me to the core if you must—so that I can know you more fully. In Jesus' name I pray. Amen.*

Thought for the Day: A proper regard for God puts everything in perspective.

60
NATIVE LANGUAGE

Psalm 98

Shout for joy to the LORD, all the earth,
burst into jubilant song with music.
—Ps. 98:4

What if all the earth acknowledged God at the same time? What would that look like? Of course, we know the day is coming when that will happen. Proper respect, regard, and love for God put everything in its right perspective. We begin to see God for who He is. And we see creation and the world around us—including evil—for what it is.

We recently attended the Bat Mitzvah—the Jewish rite of womanhood—for our daughter's friend. As we entered the synagogue, there was a tangible sense of excitement in the air. Several members of that congregation offered to lead us, as Gentiles, through the service itself. All was coupled with a perceptible reverence for this ancient tradition. The ceremony itself was beautiful. The respect for the Torah was moving, and the amount of scripture involved was inspiring.

But the music was incredible! Not the quality of the singing necessarily, but the sheer amount of it. Songs were sung following each section of the service or after each portion of scripture was read. As a friend remarked, "It's as if on hearing the Word of God the people just can't help but sing!"

I think that was Paul's thinking when he wrote,

> Do not get drunk on wine, which leads to debauchery. Instead, be filled with the Spirit. Speak to one another with psalms, hymns and spiritual songs. Sing and make music in your heart to the Lord, always giving thanks to God the Father for everything in the name of our Lord Jesus Christ (Eph. 5:18-20).

For years I've thought of this passage as a good basis for stylistically balanced worship, and I suppose it is. But deeper than that is the mandate to allow ourselves permission to respond to the Spirit's filling with the most exalted language of all—music.

Prayer: *O God, thank you for the gift of your Spirit, who fills us to overflowing. May our response be one of grateful praise through our joyful song. In Jesus' name we pray. Amen.*

Thought for the Day: As the Spirit fills, the heart sings!

61

WHAT IF . . .

Psalm 100

Know that the LORD is God. It is he who made us, and we are his.
—Ps. 100:3

Thanksgiving is at the heart of worship. Can you visualize the ancient Hebrews taking this psalm literally? Can you hear them shout? Can you see their gladness? Can you absorb their joyful songs? Like our earlier reading from Ps. 95, today's reading issues a call to worship and encourages physical activity as a response. And, of course, the reminder of God's faithfulness and enduring love propels all this.

What would church be like if we did the same today? What if we approached the parking lot with thanksgiving instead of grumbling about the lack of parking spaces? What if we entered the front doors with praise instead of idle chatter? What if we constantly lauded His name rather than the accomplishments of our favorite athletic organization? Fellowship is a part of what we believers do when we gather, but it's not the central focus of worship. What if we really took to heart the admonitions of Ps. 100? How would that change worship in your church?

Two things jump out at me as I read this passage. The first is a reminder of how we tend to water down and tame the words of Scripture. We want them to fit comfortably and unobtrusively into our lifestyle. But worship for the ancient Hebrews was anything but tame! It was all-out and uninhibited. For instance, the phrase translated "shout for joy" in verse 1 is the Hebrew word *ruwa*, which indicates "to split the ears with sound." No quiet observance for these people! Psalm 100 was a celebration of very audible proportions.

Secondly, the writer of Ps. 100 chooses to refer to his maker in two distinct ways. Verse 1 speaks of the LORD—*Yahweh*, the covenant-maker who has an active, personal relationship with His people as a whole and with individuals. Then, in verse 3, the Lord is identified as God—Elohim, the creator and sustainer of the universe, the same Elohim of Gen. 1.

What a comfort to know that the God we praise with thanksgiving is our creator! He knows us thoroughly and loves us totally. He's initiated a covenant relationship with us through His Son, Jesus. And this covenant of love and faithfulness will endure forever.

Prayer: *O Lord of goodness and faithfulness, forgive me for shrinking from a wholehearted response to you, my creator and my covenant God. I worship you with gladness and joy today. In your Son's name I pray. Amen.*

Thought for the Day: When you think of all that's good, give your thanks to God.

62

A LIVING TESTIMONY

Psalm 102

The children of your servants will live in your presence;
their descendants will be established before you.
—Ps. 102:28

My wife and I have four children. They can hardly believe that I made it through college without a cell phone, a computer, a DVD player, or even a calculator. (That last one is because I don't do math!) I'll stop before I reveal too much about my age, but you get the idea. They're amazed that I ever got anything done.

Not that they spend that much time thinking about it. They have lives of their own. One son is musically gifted, showing great promise in that field for the future. Another son demonstrates outstanding athletic prowess, and that's likely to be his career. A third son—well, he has a personality that won't stop, and that boosts his leadership skills on the ball field and in the classroom. And our daughter? She's "queen of the world," and when she's not kicking a soccer ball, she's consoling a friend or participating in a youth group Bible study. Do I sound like a proud dad here?

So much has changed since I was a kid that I can't begin to fathom what the world will be like when my four children become parents themselves. There are some things I hope will remain constant, though:

- I hope that every chance I get to tell them about God's forgiveness, protection, and leadership all through my life will encourage them in their daily grind as they face the days ahead.
- I hope they'll see that though technology has changed the world they live in, the fundamental problems we all face and the solutions to these problems are pretty basic—as old as history itself.

- I hope they'll understand that their dad didn't have all the answers, but he did know the One who does.
- I hope they'll fully grasp that as much as their mother and I love and accept them, there is One whose love for them is far greater than any of us could imagine.

Prayer: *Father, how grateful I am for the privilege of being your son! May my testimony of your goodness be passed on to the generations who follow me. In Christ's name I pray. Amen.*

Thought for the Day: Vastly rewarding to those who follow is our testimony about God.

63
BLESSED SO WE CAN BLESS

Psalm 103

Praise the LORD, O my soul;
all my inmost being, praise his holy name.
—Ps. 103:1

As we continue with the theme of giving thanks, it's important that we understand the context of verse 1 in today's reading. Many translations render the opening as "Bless the LORD, O my soul." That begs the question "If we claim that God blesses us as only He can, how in the world can we bless God, who needs nothing?" I'm convinced that our understanding is complete only when we realize that the word we read as "bless" in our Bibles may have come from one of two or three original words.

"Bless," in verse 1, is derived from *barak*, which means "to kneel down" or "to praise or salute." It's closely related to the way Mary was called "blessed" in Luke 1:42. That word in Greek is *eulogio*, "to speak well of," and is the basis of our word "eulogy." Speaking well of God is blessing Him.

That's quite different from the way God blesses us. In that context, "blessed" is more closely akin to the Greek word *makarizo*, which refers to God indwelling us as we ask Him to take part in our lives and interact in our plans. And how does God bless us most?

He forgives our sins and heals our diseases (v. 3).

He crowns us with love and compassion (v. 4).

He satisfies our desires with good things (v. 5).

He works righteousness and justice for us (v. 6).

He does not treat us according to what we deserve (v. 10).

He does not repay us according to our iniquities (v. 10).

He removes our transgressions from us (v. 12).

No wonder we want to bless Him! Those of us who have been forgiven have all the more reason to love and bless God with all that's in us. I love the old anonymous poem below, and I rely on its theology daily:

> I hear the accuser roar
> Of evils I have done.
> I know them well, and thousands more;
> Jehovah knoweth none.

Prayer: *Jehovah Rapha, healer of my spirit and soul, how I bless you today! You have redeemed and restored me, and I will bless you as long as I live. In Jesus' precious name I pray. Amen.*

Thought for the Day: For the blessings of God we should gladly bless God.

64

SPLENDOR AND MAJESTY

Psalm 104

How many are your works, O LORD!
In wisdom you made them all.
—Ps. 104:24

God's creativity is fantastic. Not only has He created all there is—He cares for and governs it. He hasn't stepped back from what He made. His providence includes sustaining and maintaining.

Part of that includes me! I want to be—like creation around me—an undeniable and natural fingerprint of God.

We do ourselves and our congregations a disservice when we neglect the artistic beauty, the poetic purity, and the theological depth of some of our classic hymns. I'm not talking style issues here—simply the incredible way God has moved men and women in the past to express their response to the magnitude of creation and the truths of Scripture.

For instance, where would we be without this hymn?

> I sing the mighty pow'r of God
>   That made the mountains rise,
> That spread the flowing seas abroad
>   And built the lofty skies.
> I sing the wisdom that ordained
>   The sun to rule the day;
> The moon shines full at His command
>   And all the stars obey.
>
> I sing the goodness of the Lord
>   That filled the earth with food;
> He formed the creatures with His word
>   And then pronounced them good.

Lord, how Thy wonders are displayed
Where'er I turn my eye:
If I survey the ground I tread
Or gaze upon the sky.

Isaac Watts

Or—

Immortal, invisible, God only wise,
In light inaccessible hid from our eyes,
Most blessed, most glorious, the Ancient of Days,
Almighty, victorious—Thy great name we praise.

Unresting, unhasting, and silent as light,
Nor wanting, nor wasting, Thou rulest in might;
Thy justice, like mountains, high soaring above
Thy clouds, which are fountains of goodness and love.

Walter Chalmers Smith

Then there's this one:

The God of Abr'ham praise,
Who reigns enthroned above,
The Ancient of eternal days,
And God of love.
Jehovah, great I AM,
By earth and heav'n confessed:
We bow and bless the sacred name
Forever blessed.

Thomas Olivers

And how about this one?

O worship the King, all glorious above,
And gratefully sing His wonderful love;
Our Shield and Defender, the Ancient of Days,
Pavilioned in splendor and girded with praise.
O tell of His might, and sing of His grace,
Whose robe is the light, whose canopy space.
His chariots of wrath the deep thunder clouds form,
And dark is His path on the wings of the storm.

Robert Grant.

Sometimes I like to go back and read these hymn texts devotionally, slowly taking in their wonderful content. I'm enriched by their beauty and inspired by their clarity. It's just a reminder to me of what an awesome Creator our God is—as if looking around me at the universe I see isn't enough!

Prayer: *"Awesome," "majestic," and "wonderful" don't really come close to describing you or your creation, Lord. But just as the seas roar and the trees of the field clap their hands, I want to applaud your greatness today. In Christ's name I pray. Amen.*

Thought for the Day: In wisdom He made us. In love He sustains us.

65

A FAMILY RESEMBLANCE

Psalm 105

Let the hearts of those who seek the LORD rejoice.
—Ps. 105:3

When we "glory in [God's] holy name" (v. 3), we not only honor God, but we also celebrate our identity in Him. Seeking Him—being what we are intended to be in Him—is fulfilling and causes our hearts to rejoice. Recounting His faithfulness and power in the past gives us confidence for today.

The word "glory," which we see in verse 3 of today's psalm, is an intriguing word. The original Hebrew word is *halal*, and it can mean "to be clear in sound, to shine, to make a show, to boast." It even has the implication of "being clamorously foolish."

With two children away at college, my wife and I find it's always good to get them home, even if it's just for the weekend. Once we're all reunited, it begins: a little bit of catching up, some good-natured ribbing, and a lot of laughs. If anyone were to spy on our little gatherings, we would no doubt be labeled "clamorously foolish."

Those who bear our family name have a lot to remember also. There's a lot of history in our family—some of it good, some not so much. I imagine it's the same with your family. But we've learned plenty from the past—mostly how God has led us, protected us, forgiven us, and loved us. It's good to look back on these times just as it's good to celebrate the now.

I think that's the point the writer of Ps. 105 was trying to make. Those of us in the family of God have lots to remember and lots to celebrate. We who bear His name can be clear about it, we can make a show because of it, we can boast in it. It's not because of anything we've done or could do, but because we recognize our bloodline, and we bear the unmistakable image and likeness of our Father.

Prayer: *Father, thank you for my family and the joy each member brings. And thank you for the undeniable honor of being called your child. In your Son's name I pray. Amen.*

Thought for the Day: As children of our Heavenly Father, we glory in His holy name.

66
SPIRITUAL AMNESIA

Psalm 106

Who can proclaim the mighty acts of the LORD or fully declare his praise?
—Ps. 106:2

How often I forget what God has done! I forget His deliverance, His mercy, and His grace. Sometimes I trample on His goodness by my selfish actions. I fear that I, too, have "put God to the test" (v. 14).

Not that it justifies my attitudes and actions, but apparently I'm not alone in this. "Selective memory" seems to be an age-old dilemma. Many think that the writer of Ps. 106 was a Levite writing in Jerusalem after the return of the Babylonian exiles. And that makes sense, because the events listed begin with Israel's slavery in Egypt, move through their exodus, and include references to their Babylonian captivity. Sadly, in each case there are also references to their rebellion, due in large part, I'm convinced, to their spiritual amnesia.

But before we shake our heads in amazement at their disbelief, we would do well to reflect on our own behavior. Aren't we also guilty at times of forgetting past deliverances? Haven't we, too, rebelled against the Spirit of God when His loving discipline has seemed too harsh to us? And haven't we at some time failed to see His hand of protection when His divine rescue didn't look the way we thought it would?

While dwelling on past failures is generally unproductive, a healthy dose of remembering our deliverance can and should point us to our Deliverer. God help us to remember all He is and all He's done.

And God help us when we forget.

Prayer: *Father, your work in my life has been loving, caring, merciful, and at times stern and disciplining. Help me never forget that above all, you are my deliverer. In Jesus' name I pray. Amen.*

Thought for the Day: Memories of yesterday's victories bring confidence for today's challenges.

67

EXPRESSION DEEPENS IMPRESSION

Psalm 107

Let them give thanks to the LORD for his unfailing love
and his wonderful deeds for men.
—Ps. 107:8

Our lives need a refrain, a chorus we can sing and turn to over and over that reaffirms our basic core beliefs. "Give thanks to the LORD for his unfailing love and his wonderful deeds for men" is a worthy refrain for our lives. We find it here in verse 8 and repeated in verses 15, 21, and 31. I think the author of this psalm knew that repetition breeds familiarity, and familiarity breeds trust.

As we continue on the topic of thanksgiving, it might be helpful to recall that living with a grateful attitude puts things into perspective: God is God; and we're not. What we've been delivered from is because of Him. The only good that's in us now is because of Him. And any godly potential for our future is because of Him. As we view life through the lens of gratitude for God's grace, then words of praise become the natural overflow of our hearts. And the more we speak them, the more we see His hand in everything. Expression deepens impression.

Psalm 107 offers two categories of blessing we would do well to recognize, acknowledge, and be grateful for. First, there's the blessing of His hand. His provision (vv. 9, 37-38) and His protection (vv. 14, 28-29) are sure indicators that His hand is on us. I'm reminded of an earlier psalm, Ps. 16, in which David said, "LORD, you have assigned me my portion and my cup; you have made my lot secure. The boundary lines have fallen for me in pleasant places; surely I have a delightful inheritance" (vv. 5-6).

Psalm 107 speaks directly to the blessing of His Word in verse 20. God's Word is His primary means of healing and restoration.

The written word reveals to us the living Word. The written word informs, instructs, and convicts us so that we become conformed to the living Word. Sharper than a two-edged sword (Heb. 4:12), the Word of God judges our thoughts and attitudes, bringing them in line with the mind of Christ. The Word of God reveals to us who God is.

Prayer: *O God, how grateful I am for your Word, which instructs me, and especially for your Son, Jesus, the Word, who has saved me! May my life-song be one of thanksgiving and praise. In your Son's name I pray. Amen.*

Thought for the Day: Life is not meant to be taken for granted, but with gratitude.

68
THE GREATER GLORY

Psalm 108

Awake, harp and lyre! I will awaken the dawn.
—Ps. 108:2

Starting the day—awaking the dawn—with God's Word gives me the right balance for the day and the right filter through which to see the world. Maybe the truth is that regular repetition of this discipline, the recitation of the "refrain," like the one we saw in Ps. 107, is the stability I need for an ever-changing world.

Today's psalm contains an echo of Ps. 57, especially in what we read in verse 5: "Be exalted, O God, above the heavens; let your glory be over all the earth." If we could interview David, he just might claim this as his own life's refrain. He was a man with an artistic soul, full of passion. He was a man of notable victories and a man of well-documented failures. Yet he was, after all, a man after God's own heart (1 Sam. 13:14), and I'm inclined to believe that David's chief end was to see Him glorified.

This is an important consideration for us as well. It's been said that when life gives us bumps, what spills out is what's truly in our hearts. If we don't get the recognition in our job or ministry that we think we deserve—is God glorified in our acceptance of this? Cruel, unkind, or untrue words are spoken of us—is God glorified in our reaction? We face an unexpected crisis in our health, our finances, or our relationships—is God glorified in our response?

This may be even a little tougher: We're suddenly blessed with a measure of professional success, financial security, or relational acceptance. Will God also be glorified in how we handle this?

Let's backtrack just a moment before we leave Ps. 108. When we read in verse 1, "I will sing and make music with all my soul," we need to know that the phrase literally means "with all my glory." That phrase means "my honor" or "my prevailings." "Heaviness" is another possible definition, meaning the weight of all the good that's happened to me. Copiousness. Abundance.

That can be hard, can't it? Remembering God when everything's going right may be more of a challenge than crying out to Him when the world seems to be falling apart. But I think I hear David reminding us that our temporal, passing "glory" is only for the purpose of reflecting His eternal glory.

Prayer: *O Lord, your love and faithfulness are beyond my understanding. I choose today to glorify you no matter what comes my way. In Christ's name I pray. Amen.*

Thought for the Day: Beyond all, in spite of all, and because of all, God is to be glorified *above* all.

69
BROTHERHOOD AND TIES THAT BIND

Psalm 109

With my mouth I will greatly extol the LORD;
in the great throng I will praise him.
—Ps. 109:30

Let's all admit it up front—Ps. 109 is not a happy psalm. The call here for punishment probably feels a little extreme to us. But then again, maybe we've all felt this way at one time or another without actually articulating it. Ah, such can be the nature of friendship when human nature sneaks in!

I don't want to live a suspicious, paranoid life, but it's obvious to me now that I really should be careful in choosing my friends. I also have to be careful to treat them in the way I would want—and may someday need—to be treated.

Most of my good friends live within a few miles of me, but some whom I love a lot live in other cities several states away. One of my very best friends actually lives on another continent! These brothers know all about me and choose to love me anyway. The ties that bind us when God brings us together are truly amazing.

If you, like me, have been blessed with a few close friends, thank God. If you've been stung by words or actions of friends, pray for a forgiving and grace-filled spirit. If you're sensing the need for a few close companions with whom to share life, ask our Father. He delights in giving good things to His children.

And be assured that you'll never find a closer, truer friend than the giver himself.

Prayer: *Jesus, friend of sinners, thank you for your abiding friendship. I am blessed to have relationships that come straight from you. In Jesus' name I pray. Amen.*

Thought for the Day: True friendship is one of God's great graces.

70

A REALITY CHECK

Psalm 113

From the rising of the sun to the place where it sets,
the name of the LORD is to be praised.
—Ps. 113:3

When God is acknowledged everywhere and in everything, then we see true reality—God for who He is, doing all He does. It's astounding to think that the Creator stoops down to care about me (v. 6).

Psalm 113 and its follow-up, Ps. 114, are other excellent reminders of God's goodness and power, bringing confidence, gratitude, and assurance to our lives. I see Ps. 113 as being divided into three sections:

Verses 1-3: God's command to praise

Verses 4-6: God's reason to praise

Verses 7-9: God's legacy to us

To my way of thinking, this is a remarkable and solid way to live our lives.

I believe that when God calls us to a task, or when He's assured us of His working in our lives, we can and should begin praising Him even before the task is fulfilled or His work is accomplished. Just think of Mary, the mother of Jesus, and her outburst of praise, the Magnificat, in Luke 1:46-55. Her response to the angel's announcement was a pure, honest exaltation of her Savior. All this, even though the earthly process had just begun and she had, I'm sure, many questions.

What has God called you to do? How has He begun working in your life? Begin right now to praise Him.

Prayer: *O God, today, all day, I will praise you for who you are and all you're doing. Help me see you in everything and trust you when my vision is not so clear. In Christ's name I pray. Amen.*

Thought for the Day: We can praise God's name even before we can see His hand.

71
CALL AND RESPONSE

Psalms 116 & 117

Because he turned his ear to me,
I will call on him as long as I live.
—Ps. 116:2

Today's reading encompasses two psalms, principally because Ps. 117 is sort of a benediction or concluding remark to Ps. 116. There's something beautiful and powerful about seeing others responding gratefully and honestly to God. I want that freedom in my worship, both pubic and private. I want to be able to articulate, personally and specifically, what He's done for me. And I want to lead in worship by being a worshiper first.

We don't really know who wrote Ps. 116. Some scholars speculate it was the work of an unnamed king of Israel. A few have gone so far as to suggest it was composed by King Hezekiah. It does bear some resemblance to his prayer of thanksgiving in Isa. 38. That aside, I love the way that once again we see God's Word expressed in the gritty, unvarnished chaos that life can be. Can you imagine one of today's rulers or political authorities expressing himself or herself like this?

One common theme we see throughout this passage is "calling on God."

> I will call on him as long as I live (v. 2).
> Then I called on the name of the LORD (v. 4)
> and call on the name of the LORD (v. 13)
> and call on the name of the Lord (v. 17).

There are plenty of experts who would speak into our lives when the cords of death entangle us or we're overcome by trouble and sorrow (v. 3). You can see them on television or hear them on the radio around the clock. Or, if you would prefer, just pay a visit to the self-help section of your favorite bookstore. You'll have plenty of offers. But there's only one who is gracious—unbelievably forgiving, righteous—with total authority and full of compassion, unending in love.

This is why I think the writer of Ps. 116 declares in verse 13, "I will lift up the cup of salvation and call on the name of the LORD." The word translated "salvation" in our Bibles indicates "deliverance, help, something saved." It's closely associated with another Hebrew word meaning "freed, rescued, preserved."

The word itself? *Yshuwah*.

The Hebrews derived the name "Joshua" from it. Later the Greek language would pronounce it "Jesus."

The next time you gather for worship, the next time life begins to close in on you, or the next time you really, really need help, who will you lift up? Who will you call on?

Prayer: *Jesus, you are salvation, deliverance, and freedom. Above all things, I lift you up in worship today. In your powerful name I pray. Amen.*

Thought for the Day: God hears every call and is lifted up on every word of praise.

72
GUIDELINES, BOUNDARIES, AND LIBERTY

Psalm 119:1-16

I delight in your decrees; I will not neglect your word.
—Ps. 119:16

The quality of my life is best judged by its adherence to the Word of God. Disciplined study results in a love for the Scriptures, and God's Word is my heritage, my treasured possession, my very life. It guides me and convicts me. It's a shield when I'm persecuted or unfairly criticized.

God's Word is also a reflection of Him: eternal, faithful, enduring. Along with soaking up the truths of Scripture, a prayer for discernment and wisdom is always a good thing. No self-help or executive management or positive thinking book can compare with God's Word.

For the next few days we'll be looking at portions of Ps. 119, the longest chapter in the Bible as well as unapologetic honoring of the precepts of God. In many ways, it's like a proverb, an instructional manual on upright and godly living. And it all begins with a holy reverence for the utterances of God.

This whole chapter is full of what on first inspection sounds like legal jargon. Terms like "law," "statutes," "precepts," "decrees," and "commands" sound as if we should be up to our necks in dos and don'ts. But on closer examination, we'll see that all this is intended not only to make life on earth more pleasant but also to ultimately strengthen our relationship with God himself. Speaking to God, the psalmist writes, "I have hidden your word in my heart that I might not sin against you" (v. 11).

Let's make that our aim as well.

Prayer: *Father, as I meditate on and delight in your precepts, draw me not only to your word but also to your heart. In Jesus' name I pray. Amen.*

Thought for the Day: God's guidelines and boundaries give us our liberty.

73
THROUGH THE LENS OF SCRIPTURE

Psalm 119:33-48

Give me understanding, and I will keep your law
and obey it with all my heart.

—Ps. 119:34

I am so grateful for the biblical training I received as a child. In the church I attended as a youth, we all went through—or endured—a few years of fairly intense study that included an overview of the Bible, a large number of memorized verses, and a method of reciting all the books of the Bible in order. "Sword drill," we called it, and I'll be forever thankful for the foundations it laid in my life.

But knowledge *about* God's Word is not the same thing as allowing it to penetrate the spirit. Facts are useless without some sort of application. My father used to say to me, his trivia-buff middle child: "Marty, you've got a head full of knowledge nobody wants!" Memorization is meaningless unless I apply it to my life.

I think that's what the writer of Ps. 119 had in mind when he wrote, "Teach me" (v. 33); "Give me understanding" (v. 34); "Direct me" (v. 35); "Turn my heart" (v. 36); and "Turn my eyes" (v. 37). It's the "give me understanding" part that really intrigues me, and it's a concept I want in my life. The Hebrew word *biyn* (translated "understanding") means "to distinguish, to separate mentally, to consider, to discern, to be cunning." In other words, it's to view the world through the lens of Scripture, to make decisions based on an intuitive sense that's informed and directed by God's Word.

A few years back I wrote a piece for a publication that was really picky about accurately referencing each and every biblical quote. Once the piece was in print, I realized I had quoted a passage without referencing it. In fact, I didn't even realize at first that I was quoting at all. These particular verses had become so ingrained that they were part of my everyday speech. At first I thought, *How could I have missed this?* Then it came to me—*Thank you, God, that your Word is this deeply burned into me, so much so that I have trouble sometimes discerning if it's you or me talking.*

I don't know about you, but I want God's Word to so infiltrate me that every thought, decision, action, and attitude is defined and guided by these wonderful precepts we've been given. A tall order, but so worth the diligence.

Prayer: *O God, today I ask that you teach me, direct me, and turn my heart and eyes to you. Give me understanding of your Word so that I may know you. In Jesus' name I pray. Amen.*

Thought for the Day: More than just knowledge, God's Word gives life.

74
PROFIT IN SUFFERING

Psalm 119:57-72

It was good for me to be afflicted
so that I might learn your decrees.
—Ps. 119:71

There's profit to be gained through our suffering. Just as a surgeon's knife can excise a cancerous tumor or repair an artery, the scalpel of God's Word brings healing and restoration. Though painful, God's truth will, if we allow it, cut through our spiritual and moral cancer, bringing healing, health, and wholeness.

However, this doesn't just happen. A young mother was pleasantly surprised when she walked into her four-year-old son's suddenly neat and tidy bedroom. When she asked about how that happened, the child replied, "It didn't just happen—I *happened* it!" The same is true for us in our terminal condition called "humanity." For God's Word to do its healing, restorative work, we must allow it into our lives, give it permission to poke and prod, then permit it to cut away all that is not God-honoring.

Spiritual, scriptural surgery is usually painful. Still, it's the only way to be what we're called to be. Centuries after the writing of this psalm, the author of the Book of Hebrews put it this way: "The word of God is living and active. Sharper than any double-edged sword, it penetrates even to dividing soul and spirit, joints and marrow; it judges the thoughts and attitudes of the heart" (Heb. 4:12).

Is it time to schedule some surgery today? If so, please get to it. Your health depends on it.

Prayer: *Lord, you are the divine surgeon and great physician. You are the God who heals me. I will allow your Word to penetrate and heal me today. In Jesus' name I pray. Amen.*

Thought for the Day: Pain makes us think; thinking makes us wise; wisdom makes life profitable.

75
A LAMP AND A LIGHT

Psalm 119:80-112

Your word is a lamp to my feet and a light to my path.
—Ps. 119:105

It's no accident that today's highlighted verse includes the words "lamp" and "light." A lamp illuminates what is immediately around us, but light exposes much, much more than merely our proximity. "A lamp to my feet" means my present circumstances. "A light to my path" means my future. That's it! God's Word is my guide for both today *and* tomorrow.

There are some time-oriented phrases in this portion of Ps. 119 that are worth noting, because they remind us that God's Word—indeed, God himself—is beyond our normal, finite concept of time.

- "Your word, O LORD, is eternal" (v. 89).
- "Your faithfulness continues through all generations" (v. 90).
- "Your laws endure to this day" (v. 91).
- "Your commands are boundless" (v. 96).

I see something more personal than these time-oriented concepts. I see concepts that lead to wisdom and understanding for me, concepts that speak of insight leading to obedience, concepts that direct me to a loving Father. It's as if He's saying, *Child, if you'll just hear my word and follow my lead, I'll give you more than head knowledge, more than even a proper understanding. I'll give you me.*

Prayer: *Father, that's what I really want— just you. In my understanding of your Word, allow me a glimpse into your heart. In Jesus' name I pray. Amen.*

Thought for the Day: Though heaven and earth will pass away, God's Word will remain eternal.

76
HANDLE WITH CARE

Psalm 119:145-160

My eyes stay open through the watches of the night,
that I may meditate on your promises.
—Ps. 119:148

It's been said that you can justify most any point about most anything by misapplying some portion of Scripture. I suppose that's true. We've all heard the story of the distraught man who found himself in deep trouble personally and financially. In a frantic search for help, he decided to open his Bible at random, point blindly to a verse, then follow its directives. To his horror, when he opened his eyes, he found that his finger had landed on Matt. 27:5, which, speaking of Judas, says, "Then he went away and hanged himself."

Not exactly what any of us would call properly handling the Scriptures, is it? And that's why it's so vitally important that we don't simply read through God's Word in a casual manner but rather dig in, reading different versions occasionally for insight, studying comments wise scholars have made, and ultimately comparing scripture with scripture.

Centuries after Ps. 119 was composed, the apostle Paul wisely advised his young protégé, Timothy: "Do your best to present yourself to God as one approved, a workman who does not need to be ashamed and who correctly handles the word of truth" (2 Tim. 2:15).

God's Word—eternal, enduring, and priceless.

Prayer: *O God, may I see your Word for all that it is as I grow in knowledge and understanding of all you are. Breathe into me your very Word that I might have life in you. In Jesus' name I pray. Amen.*

Thought for the Day: The riches of God's Word deserve careful, protective handling.

77

OUR SPIRITUAL DNA

Psalms 121 & 122

I rejoiced with those who said to me, "Let us go to the house of the LORD."
—Ps. 122:1

Today's reading from the Word involves two psalms because of their shared historical background and because of their similar present-day application. Both are subtitled "A song of ascents." Most likely this means they were ceremonial or liturgical songs the Hebrews sang as they "ascended" the steps of the Temple in Jerusalem, or as they approached the geographical elevation of the holy city itself.

Psalm 121 focuses on God's protection, while Ps. 122 speaks to the joy of fellowship and worship with others. It's a good thing to repeat affirmations of God's attributes when we get together with likeminded believers. Even when we've assembled with those with whom we have minor doctrinal or theological differences, acknowledging God's goodness is common ground and should be familiar, comfortable territory. We need modern-day songs of ascents.

When the Church really is the Church, doing and behaving as it should—"firing on all cylinders," as a friend of mine says—then there's nothing like it. And there's nothing like the sheer joy and raw power of gathering with other believers. God made us to need each other, and we need to honor our maker's intentions. It's in our spiritual DNA to gravitate toward our Creator and to do it together.

Prayer: *Maker of heaven and earth, how I delight in your creation! Thank you for the privilege of serving you alongside these fellow believers. We lift our hearts to you. In Jesus' name I pray. Amen.*

Thought for the Day: There's nothing like the Church, and no one like our God.

78

EVERY MOVE YOU MAKE

Psalm 125

As the mountains surround Jerusalem,
so the LORD surrounds his people both now and forevermore.
—Ps. 125:2

When you're surrounded by God, every move you make must go through Him. No thought, word, or action proceeds from us without first going through the filter of God's presence. And no attack of the enemy will assault us without first being sifted through His hand.

I've come to the conclusion that we're sifted, as Peter was in Luke 22:31, when we need sifting. My experience has been that there's much to be learned when we go through perilous times. If we'll pay attention, we'll learn an enormous amount about ourselves and, better yet, about God.

Usually an attack of the enemy is intensified, because it hits us right where we're most vulnerable. Financial pressures, health issues, moral problems—these are sometimes overwhelming, because in some inexplicable way, that's where our sense of security and self-esteem is founded. And that's why we become victims of an ungodly oppression.

We often fight back, don't we? *What is God teaching me?* is replaced with *How could this happen to me?* The good news is that sometimes God will completely change a situation so that no remnant of evil remains (v. 3). We won't be tempted to use the weapons we abhor in self-protective retaliation.

So as you move through this day, no matter what pours out of you or what external forces assail you, remember—you've been surrounded.

Prayer: *God, you are my refuge, my security, my stronghold. No matter what comes my way today, I'll see it as an opportunity to grow more into your likeness. In your Son's name I pray. Amen.*

Thought for the Day: Trials and blessings alike mold us into godly character.

79

REAPING WHAT WE DON'T SOW

Psalms 126, 127, & 128

Those who sow in tears will reap with songs of joy.
—Ps. 126:5

I couldn't resist combining three psalms into today's reading, because all three complement each other and have one overarching, universal theme: we reap what we sow.

That's good news and bad news, right? Those of us still in the childrearing years feel this in an especially acute way. Sometimes the rewards of raising young ones are great. We see hints of intellectual prowess, athletic superiority, artistic ability, or even a glimmer of a Christlike character. And, of course, we're quick to take the lion's share of credit for their upbringing!

Then there are those times we observe a quality or action in our offspring and wonder in shocked disbelief where that came from. Often a glance in the mirror gives us our answer. We reap what we sow.

Occasionally, though, this axiom doesn't seem to hold true. The prophet Habakkuk had something to say about fig trees not budding, no grapes on the vines, failing crops, and fields that produce no food. Verses 17-18 of Hab. 3 mention this, as well as his mature response. And as for us today, we labor for years raising a family or in other aspects of our lives, and nothing good seems to come of it. We break our backs working with the best of intentions and see no visible results.

Be encouraged, my friend. The promise of today's Scripture reading is this: you sow in tears, you will reap with songs of joy. Your Heavenly Father mourns and weeps with you, hears your cry, and has pity. In fact, He's right beside you. Hang in there—the final verse of your life's song has not yet been sung.

Though sometimes He leads through waters deep,
  Trials fall across the way;
Though sometimes the path seems rough and steep,
  See His footprints all the way.

—Luther B. Bridgers

Prayer: O God, there are days when I feel more like crying my eyes out than singing my heart out. In those times, please remind me of your steadfast presence. In Jesus' name I pray. Amen.

Thought for the Day: Our struggle for significance apart from God's purposes is in vain.

80

A MATTER OF OPINION

Psalm 129

They have greatly oppressed me from my youth,
but they have not gained the victory over me.
—Ps. 129:2

Today's reading is another of those not-too-cheery psalms. I sincerely hope you're not discouraged by this, because, believe it or not, good news is on the way!

We all have, to some degree, detractors and troublesome people in our lives. How we respond in relation to those is far more important than anything they could say about or do to us. God's opinion about us is what really counts. And He's shared that opinion with us:

I have loved you with an everlasting love; I have drawn you with loving-kindness (*Jer.* 31:3).

Since you are precious and honored in my sight, and because I love you, I will give men in exchange for you, and people in exchange for your life (*Isa.* 43:4).

I know the plans I have for you . . . plans to prosper you and not to harm you, plans to give you hope and a future (*Jer.* 29:11).

I will show my love to the one I called "Not my loved one." I will say to those called "Not my people," "You are my people; and they will say "You are my God" (*Hosea* 2:23).

Though the mountains be shaken and the hills be removed, yet my love for you will not be shaken nor my covenant of peace be removed (*Isa.* 54:10).

It's tempting to order our lives according to the expectation and approval of those around us. And we do want to be godly examples and accurate representatives of our Savior as possible. But the truth is, there will be times when we won't please everyone, won't agree with everyone, and won't understand everyone. Nor will we be pleasing to, agreeable with, or understood by everyone. At those times, we may become the target of some pretty harsh words or deeds. Despite our best intentions, others may question our convictions. We may even question them ourselves.

When that occurs, let's step back and remember whom we're out to please. The sentiments of others aren't vital. While it is a matter of opinion, God's is the only opinion that ultimately matters.

Prayer: *Loving God, I thank you for your precious words of encouragement to me. May I live my life in response to your love, pleasing in your sight. In Christ's wonderful name I pray. Amen.*

Thought for the Day: God's opinion of us is expressed in His love toward us.

81
ARTISTIC ENDEAVORS

Psalm 132

Let us go to his dwelling place;
let us worship at his footstool.
—Ps. 132:7

Ps. 132 appears to have been written, like many of the psalms, in some sort of intentional Hebrew poetic form. As a musician, I'm so glad God chose not only to affirm and bless the arts in His Word but also to actually present portions of it in an artistic manner. When it comes to creativity, I'm amazed at the master artisan.

Throughout Scripture, it's easy to see that God had a lot to say—and still does—about the arts in worship. His instructions for the building of the Tabernacle included fabrics and fixtures designed to serve as visual, artistic reminders of himself. In fact, you'll find in Exod. 31 a reference to Bezalel, a craftsman and artistic type, who is the very first person mentioned to be filled with the Spirit of God. Further, those God ordained as musicians and priests, He did so not for the sake of music or liturgy itself but for the greater purpose of worship.

Verses 7-9 of today's reading were most likely intended to be sung by a congregation or maybe spoken as a part of a liturgy. This little litany has strong connections to 1 Chron. 28:2; 2 Chron. 6:41-42; and Ps. 99:5, 9. The Hebrew people spoke of God's throne being in heaven and His footstool on earth, more specifically on "the mountains." His "resting place" was seen as the ark of the covenant, itself an artistically elaborate, gold-covered ornate work of craftsmanship. It represented the manifest presence of God. Visual imagery was a dynamic and important concept in their understanding of God.

So what does all that mean for us today? If I understand God's Word correctly at all, He's ordained and blessed the arts, particularly those employed in worship. While I strongly believe God is behind all the creativity we can see, the highest and noblest calling of artists and craftsmen is not art for art's sake. Rather, it's in pointing us all to the original Creator himself.

Visual imagery and artistic representation of this reality—*God is with us.*

Prayer: *Lord, you are the master craftsman and the ultimate artist. My humble offerings could never compare to your immaculate greatness. Still, I want to point others to you through the gifts you've given. In Jesus' name I pray. Amen.*

Thought for the Day: Artistic expression can make a holy impression.

82

UNITY

Psalm 133

How good and pleasant it is when brothers live together in unity!
—Ps. 133:1

Most likely you've heard the story, but it addresses a core issue presented by today's psalm. Amazing, isn't it, how God could inspire writers centuries ago to pen words that would strike at the heart of matters today? And it's equally amazing how today's issues find their root cause and solution in Scripture.

A well-known religious leader from outside the United States was questioned about his faith, particularly about his disinterest in embracing Christianity. His response was something along the lines of "I would gladly consider Christianity if only I could see the followers of Jesus behaving more like Him."

Ouch! What an indictment on the Church! Surely it saddens the Father's heart when brothers and sisters do not live together in unity. I'm convinced that one of the enemy's most deceptive, wicked, and incessant schemes is causing disunity among the followers of Christ. Not only does this evil device waylay the purpose and mission of a local fellowship—it also causes the world to look with skepticism on the Church, watching us to see if our faith is really real.

Often what divides us is trivial, wouldn't you agree? Sometimes, though, there are issues that warrant our taking a stand. Things like truth and the authority of God's Word are worth defending. And again, these issues can be two of Satan's most insidious tactics. While we are called to be grace-filled in areas concerning personality, taste, style, or preference, I believe Scripture compels us to hold fast to the unchanging tenets God has laid out for us.

So what's all this about unity being like oil running down Aaron's beard? (v. 2). When Old Testament priests were consecrated, Aaron being the first, part of that ceremony included anointing their heads with oil. This was a symbol of consecration to God. (See

Exod. 29:7 and Levi. 21:10.) By likening unity to the total saturation of Aaron in the anointing oil, David is saying that we, too, are to be called into sanctification—totally set apart for God.

Unity is a work only God can do. But then, that's what the Church is all about.

Prayer: *Lord, forgive us when we allow petty things to divide us, shifting our focus away from you. Set us apart for the work you've called us to do. In Christ's name we pray. Amen.*

Thought for the Day: When we're set apart, we're less likely to fall apart.

83
IT WORKS BOTH WAYS

Psalms 134 & 135

Praise the L<small>ORD</small>, all you servants of the L<small>ORD</small>
who minister by night in the house of the L<small>ORD</small>.
—Ps. 134:1

I have a theory that most people won't go any deeper in their worship than those who lead them. I think that's because artificiality or doing things on "auto pilot" is more apparent than we would like to believe. If this is true, then it's an awesome privilege and a heavy responsibility to lead our people into an encounter with God.

I see Ps. 134 and 135 as sort of role reversal as far as worship encouragement is concerned. Psalm 134 is the concluding psalm in the "Songs of Ascent," the corporate expressions the ancient Hebrews sang with and to each other as they approached Jerusalem and the Temple of God. Psalm 135 echoes a lot of the same thoughts and even the same words of Ps. 134.

So far the psalms we've looked at that include exhortations for the worship of God have pretty-much been addressed to "the people," and we've assumed that the words were spoken by a priest or some priestly group. But these two psalms seem a little different. They're addressed to "all you servants of the L<small>ORD</small> who minister by night in the house of the L<small>ORD</small>," or "in the courts of the house of our God." They appear to be words of encouragement from the congregation to their leaders.

I wonder if Ps. 134 wasn't, in fact, a farewell song, intended to bless the Levites as the worshipers began their journey home. I can almost see and hear them as they echoed back to the priest the words they had heard so many times before: "Continue to praise God! Worship Him with everything that's in you! And may God bless you!"

You may be a worship leader or a pastor or part of a worship ministry team. You may be a "civilian" who just loves praising God.

I can tell you this with certainty—there's no greater joy for a congregation than to be led by trusted leaders whom they see as totally sold out to the worship of God. And there's no greater joy for a worship leader than to see those he or she leads responding to God with their whole hearts.

Words of encouragement in the worship of God—it works both ways.

Prayer: *Father, I'm so thankful for those who lead me in worship. Give me the opportunity to prompt and encourage them also. In the name of Christ I pray. Amen.*

Thought for the Day: Our worship of God is an encouragement to those around us.

84
LIVING ON PURPOSE

Psalm 138

The LORD *will fulfill his purpose for me.*
—Ps. 138:8

I've discovered that to engage an unbeliever in a conversation about God, I usually have to meet the unbeliever on his or her own terms. I've learned to gain acceptance through what that person values most. If I display an interest in that person, show friendship and respect, then he or she is ready to listen.

For many of us, this sort of scenario plays out most often in the workplace. When I'm interacting with musicians who don't know Jesus, my aim is to be as thoroughly and professionally prepared as possible. Whether in a rehearsal, a concert, or a recording situation, making great music is what initially binds us. After that, I pray they'll see something about the rest of me that's attractive.

I'm a firm believer that God never intended us to be isolated from the rest of the world. He needs shining lights in every arena of life. God is looking for Christian electricians, teachers, plumbers, and politicians. He can work miracles through believing accountants, artists, and musicians. Many high-profile Christ followers have been demeaned for not offering their talents exclusively to the Christian world. But that seems short-sighted to me.

How will others hear if we don't tell them? And how can we tell them if they never open themselves to hearing? You and I have a divinely ordained purpose in life and a glorious opportunity to share our incredible God. Chances are, these opportunities are right under our noses.

Prayer: *Father, I'm overwhelmed that you've created a plan and a purpose for me. Give me the vision and courage to live it out right where I am. In Jesus' name I pray. Amen.*

Thought for the Day: God often plants us right where we'll bloom best.

85

CREATED TO BE ME

Psalm 139

Search me, O God, and know my heart;
test me and know my anxious thoughts.

—Ps. 139:23

God knows all about me. That's comforting—and frightening! Why is it, then, that I feel as if I have to pretend with Him sometimes? I want our relationship to be characterized by honesty.

In light of the truth that God knows all about us, including what lies ahead, I've often wondered why He would choose to test us, as He did Abraham, Moses, and Job. Was it because He didn't know how they—or we—would react? What I've come to realize is that our testing proves things to us. Our testing reminds us of our frailty and drives us to our security.

When trials come your way, when true tragedy strikes, when life proves itself unfair, do you ever want to lash out at God? Question His authority? Challenge His sovereignty? Doubt His compassion? It's at those times I've learned to check my thoughts, my attitudes, and my motives. I can't always choose what will happen to me, but I can choose how I'll react.

Like Job, I've learned that God's ways are so much higher than mine. His thoughts are indescribably deeper than mine. His purposes for me are good, pure, and always for my best. He's "hem[med] me in" (v. 5) for my own good. His boundaries—those physical, emotional, and practical limitations—are for my freedom. I'm free to be who He created me to be, totally at liberty to live within His plan, and totally at ease realizing He knows my coming and my going, familiar with all my ways.

It seems that every week scientists discover some new facet of how the human body functions and our brains operate. Psychologists gain and share insight relating to why we behave as we do. Sociologists explore the ways we interact, peaceably or aggressively.

None of this is news to God. He formed us and knew us even before birth. In fact, He even wrote the manual on how we're to exist on this earth. Our task is to live in accordance with His plan. Our supreme goal is to conform our thoughts to His thoughts.

Prayer: *O God, forgive me for thinking and acting on my own. Fill me today with such an assurance of your presence in my life that I'll hardly know what thoughts are mine and what are yours. In Jesus' name. Amen.*

Thought for the Day: When God searches me, what will He find?

86

A FRAGRANT OFFERING

Psalm 141

May my prayer be set before you like incense;
may the lifting up of my hands
be like the evening sacrifice.
—Ps. 141:2

The intent and heart behind ancient Hebrew religious ritual is good. Like any ritual or liturgy, when it becomes rote and meaningless—tradition for tradition's sake—we're in trouble. Prayer, like incense, lifting-up of hands, sacrifice—should point us to God and not be an end in itself.

If you were to visit my church, you would see many physical gestures of worship, but the burning of incense wouldn't be one of them. In fact, for many of us in the Evangelical Christian world, the whole concept of burning incense in worship has sort of a strange and mystical quality to it. But it *is* in our heritage, so let's take a quick look at that. A little aromatherapy could do us good.

Historians tell us that the offering of incense in religious ceremonies was common among nearly all ancient civilizations, including the Babylonians, Egyptians, Assyrians, and extensively used in Jewish worship. For the Jews, it had a distinct formula, and they were instructed that it was to be sacred, holy to them. They were never to use incense for their own pleasure. (See Exod. 30:34-38.)

Incense was symbolic of the prayers of the high priest as they rose to heaven. You'll remember that in the Tabernacle and in the Temple that followed, nearly every furnishing had some symbolic meaning that pointed to God's involvement in the lives of His people. Revelation 8:3-5 underscores our understanding of "the priesthood of believers" when we read of an angel standing before the altar of God, burning incense "with the prayers of all the saints."

We're assured, by the way, that the smoke of the incense, together with the prayers of the saints, "went up before God."

There's something about a fragrant offering that pleases and honors God. Jesus himself received and approved of one woman's offering of worship as she anointed Him with an expensive perfume. You can relive that story in Matt. 26, Mark 14, or John 12. But I love the way the apostle Paul equates sacrifice with a pleasing aroma. In Eph. 5:2 he writes, "And live a life of love, just as Christ loved us and gave himself up for us as a fragrant offering and sacrifice to God." And in writing to his friends in Philippi, he assured them, "I am amply supplied, now that I have received from Epaphroditus the gifts you sent. They are a fragrant offering, an acceptable sacrifice, pleasing to God" (Phil. 4:18).

So the next time you light a candle at home, spend just a moment and let your prayer rise with the fragrance. Then offer your own sacrifice of praise.

Prayer: *Holy Father, may my prayer, like the incense of old, be a pleasing fragrance to you. May my sacrifice of praise be acceptable in your sight. In your Son's powerful name I pray. Amen.*

Thought for the Day: God is pleased by our fragrant offerings of prayer and sacrifice.

87

ALL THAT AND MORE

Psalm 144

He is my loving God and my fortress,
my stronghold and my deliverer,
my shield, in whom I take refuge.
—Ps. 144:2

God is the great rescuer, the consummate deliverer, and the ulti-mate stronghold. I think a reliance on God is at the top of my list of the things I want to leave my children. As verse 12 of today's psalm puts it, "Then our sons in their youth will be like well-nurtured plants, and our daughters will be like pillars carved to adorn a palace."

Today's key verse, verse 2, speaks of God as "my loving God." That's the *New International Version's* wording, but I decided it might be interesting to see how a few other translations rendered this title. Their interpretations:

"My goodness"—King James Version
"My Covenant Love"—*Modern Language Version*
"My steadfast love"—*Amplified Bible*
"My rock"—*Revised Standard Version*
"My lovingkindness"—*New American Standard Bible*

One commentator has suggested that the name should literally be "my unfailing love." And that makes sense. It certainly encapsu-lates all of the above and is a perfect word picture of who God has promised and proved to be. This, too, is something I hope I can leave my children—an understanding that however we view our God, there are more facets to that view than we'll ever comprehend.

If we can see our way through the battlefield language and im-agery of Ps. 144, I think we'll discover a highly relevant psalm for today. So what is it you need right now—a fortress? A stronghold? A deliverer? A shield? A refuge?

Oh, friend, He's all that—and more.

Prayer: *I praise you, God my rock, my fortress, and my stronghold. Lord, you are my deliverer and my shield. I bow before you just now. In Jesus' name I pray. Amen.*

Thought for the Day: There is no one word to describe our only God.

88

SILENCE ISN'T ALWAYS GOLDEN

Psalm 145

Let every creature praise his holy name for ever and ever.

—Ps. 145:21

Praising God in every circumstance is a choice, an act of will and determination. It's also a discipline. Psalm 145 is a great reminder of this. It begins the last section of "praise songs" from the Book of Psalms. Extolling the works and character of God keeps me mindful and aware of who He is and all He's done, making it natural for me to respond. Silence isn't always golden, you know!

Magnifying God, focusing on Him, doesn't make Him any bigger than He already is. It's our *perception* of Him that's changed. Our perspective is put in place. Our understanding becomes clearer. When a human cell is placed under a microscope, or when a star is viewed through a telescope, the cell and the star are not enlarged. It's simply that our *view* of them is enhanced.

So, too, by "magnifying" God, by exalting Him, by meditating on Him, our sense of His greatness is enlarged. As we laud His character, especially as it's expressed through His many names, our confidence in Him is increased. The inevitable result is that we proclaim His goodness, His faithfulness, and His holiness.

I've learned to love the participation of children in our worship services. Their attitude of wonder and joy is infectious. When we read, "One generation will commend your works to another" (v. 4), we generally think of adults teaching those who are younger. And there's validity in that, as Deut. 6:5-9 implores us. But I've discovered there's much to derive from the way our children lead us in worship. They have no theological hang-ups and no pride of knowledge. They simply praise a God who's far bigger and greater than they are. And so, this younger generation is commending His works to us, the older, who have so much to learn.

Prayer: *My God, so often I've made you smaller in my eyes than you really are. Help me to see you today as a great, exalted, and mighty God. And with the wonder of a child, help me praise you to every generation. In your Son's name I pray. Amen.*

Thought for the Day: How we see God affects how we see our world.

89

MY FIRST AND LAST THOUGHT

Psalm 146

I will praise the LORD all my life;
I will sing praise to my God as long as I live.
—Ps. 146:2

I want my life to be characterized as one of praise. I want my first response to life to be love for others and worship toward God.

Classic hymn writer Isaac Watts wrote,

I'll praise my Maker while I've breath;
And when my eyes shall close in death,
Praise shall employ my nobler powers.

There's a Hebrew ritual that acknowledges God as the sovereign giver of all things. The words of this ritual are recited both in the Temple and in the home, particularly in ceremonial times of thanksgiving. It begins with the words "Blessed art Thou, O Lord our God, King of the universe, for Thou hast . . ." Then, as I understand it, the sentence is completed by a listing of all the blessings of God that come to mind: family, friends, health, protection, and a multitude of others. The object is to help us see all that we have as coming from the hand of God.

Not a bad practice if you ask me. It's just natural that we would want to respond to God in worship. Praising Him should be a natural, at-home kind of experience. Let's pray that, with His help, magnifying Him will become our most instinctive personality trait.

Prayer: *O Lord, if I had a thousand tongues and a thousand lives, I could never honor you or praise you completely. Yet today I will try. In Jesus' name I pray. Amen.*

Thought for the Day: When it comes to responding to God, silence is not always golden.

90
WORSHIPING IN TUNE

Psalm 150

*Let everything that has breath praise the L*ORD.

—Ps. 150:6

We've come to the end of our journey through the Book of Psalms. There's so much of God we've discovered, yet so much more we'll never comprehend. But then, who wants a God we can fully explain or understand? We serve a God whose greatness is vast beyond our imagination. His creativity is mind-boggling in its diversity. His power is awesome! His love is everlasting! Creation shouts, "Hallelujah!"

It's fitting that today's reading closes out the Book of Psalms. Its universal call to worship addresses all of creation, heaven and earth alike, and even meanders through the orchestra and choir as it invokes worship of the Creator. Perhaps Ps. 150 was actually written as a concluding statement, a grand finale to the symphony of praise we've been living with these past days. It feels much like the conclusions of the smaller "books" within the Psalms (41:13; 72:19; 89:52; and 106:48). Only this time, it's on a grander scale, with a pounding, insistent theme: "Praise the Lord!"

As a musician, I love the sound of an orchestra playing in tune. There's something incredibly right when the subtleties of intonation are mastered. And there's something terribly jarring when they're not. I've learned to recognize out-of-tune playing not so much because I have a great ear, but more because I know what "in-tune" sounds like. And nothing else matches up.

It's the same with our worship. In-tune worship is not about flash and dazzle, musicianship and expertise, technological brilliance, or even theological depth of knowledge. In-tune worship happens when every creature engaged is focused on our Lord. Do you remember the story of Solomon bringing the ark back to the Temple in 2 Chron. 5? As part of the proceedings, a large orchestra

159

accompanied a huge choir as they praised the God of heaven. The upshot of the story is that God's glory so filled the Temple, in the form of a cloud, that the priests could not continue their ministry.

Now this is important. Read it slowly: God's glory did not fill the Temple because of the size, expertise, or volume of the music and musicians. God's glory filled the Temple because, as verse 13 of 2 Chron. 5 states, "The trumpeters and singers joined in unison, as with one voice." That's in-tune worship. Let every creature that has breath praise the Lord.

Prayer: *O God, in my worship of you, may I keep you foremost, above any distraction and beyond any triviality. I want to praise you according to your excellent greatness. In Jesus' name I pray. Amen.*

Thought for the Day: God's unequaled greatness deserves our unhindered worship.